AF254819

THE STORMY LEGACY OF WINDANSEA

Christopher Briscoe

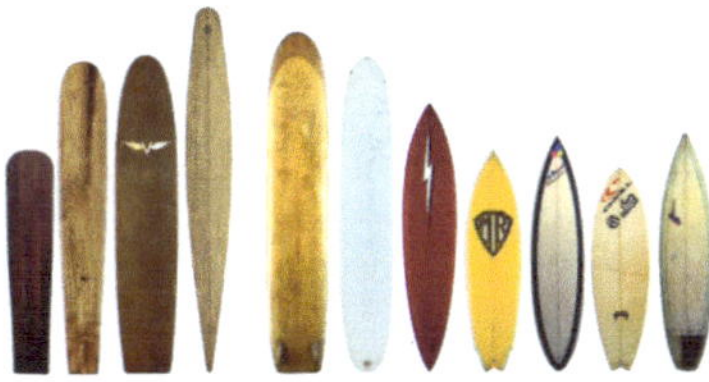

The Stormy Legacy of WindanSea

Published by: Shifting Gears Productions, Ashland, Oregon

Interior & Cover Design by: Christopher Briscoe / Align Visual Arts & Communication

ISBN: 978-0-9899404-4-3

Printed in the United States of America

"Out of the water, I am nothing."
-Duke Kahanamoku

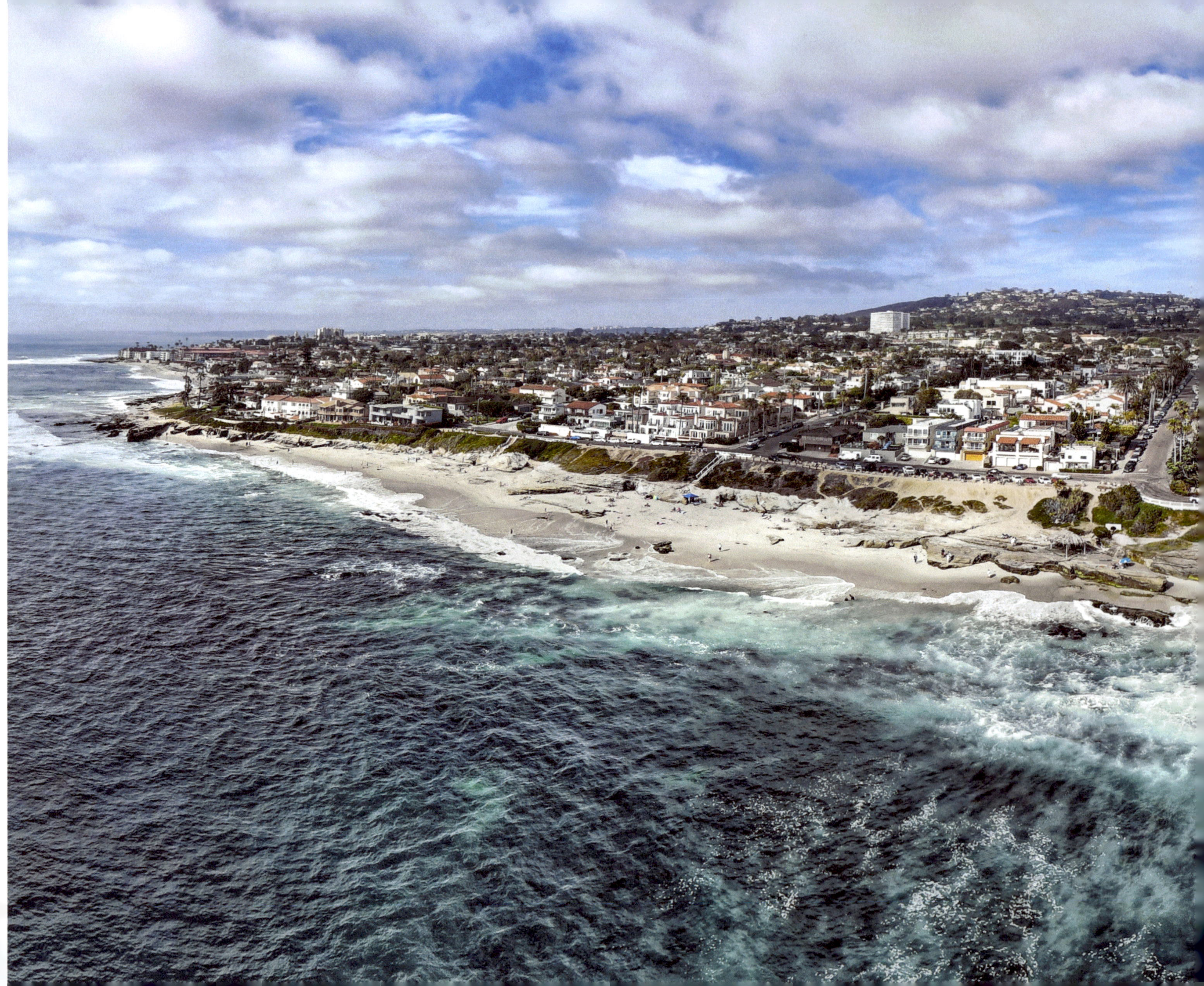

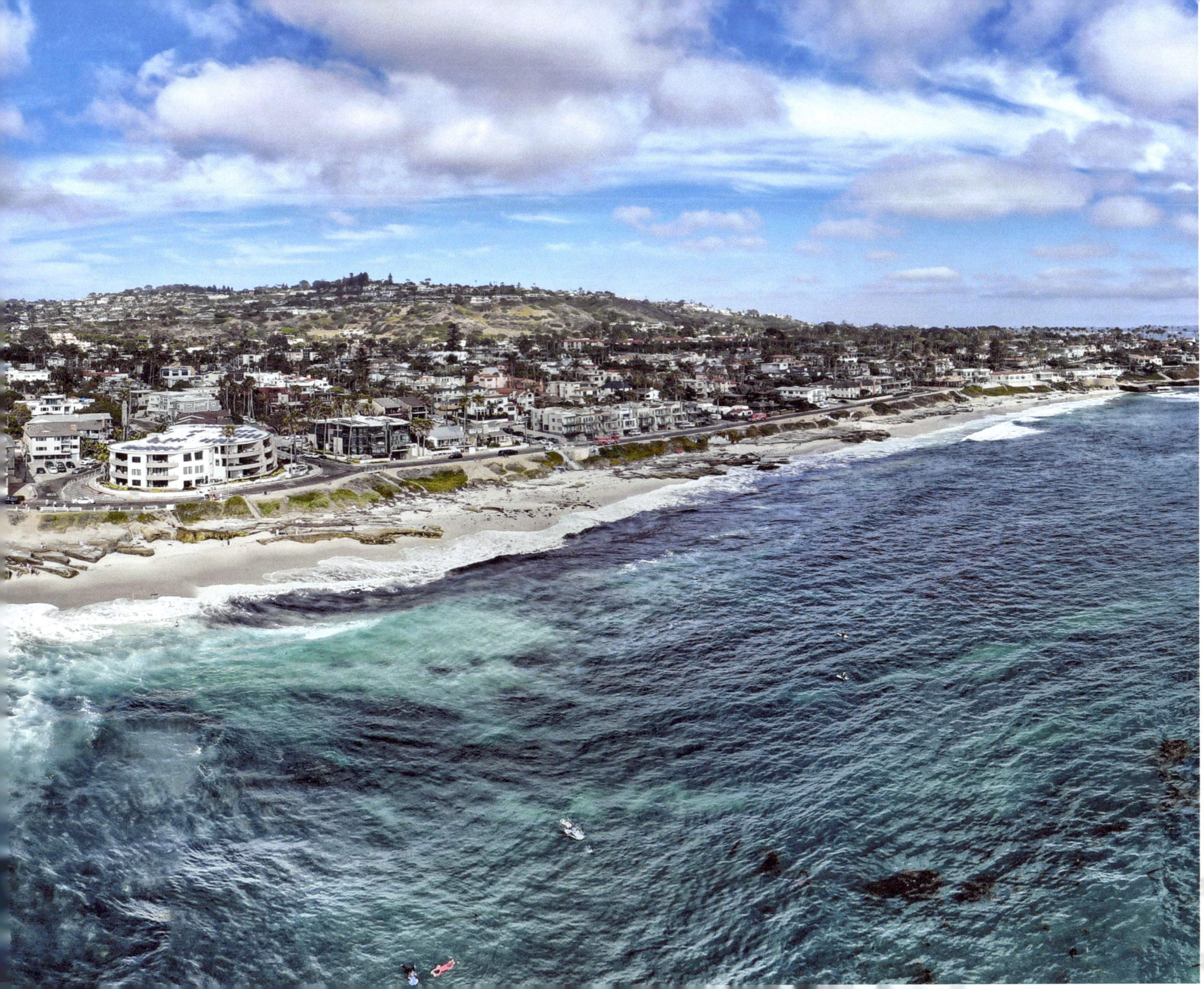

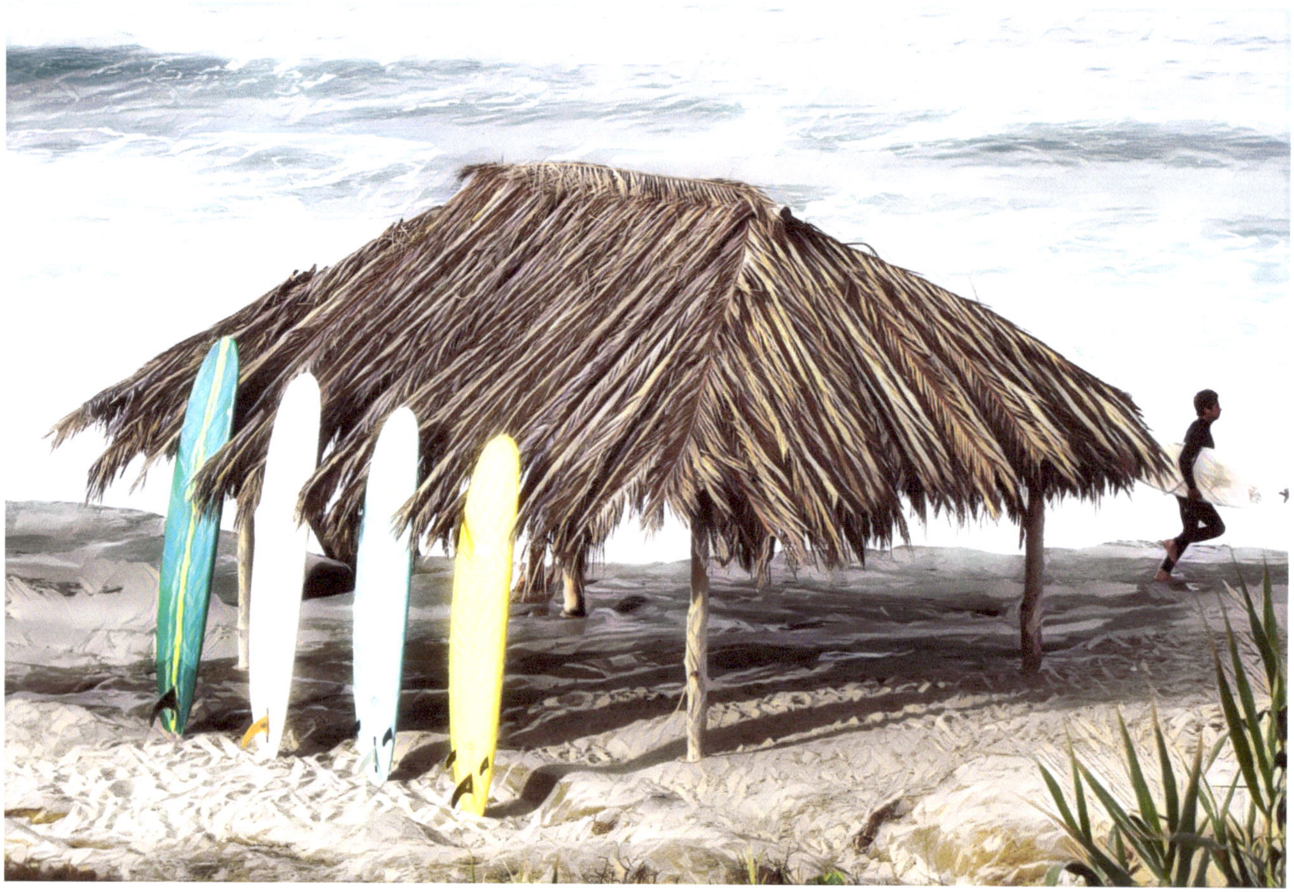

AT A GLANCE, THE LA JOLLA COASTLINE is a postcard vision: sandy coves bending around a series of tight nooks and boulders, seated below a wave-worn sandstone plateau. The crowning point along this road, aptly named Neptune Place, is a surfer's shack, made of eucalyptus poles and palm-fronds.

The shack was built in 1946 by 3 friends: Woody Ekstrom, Fred Kenyon and Don Okey, anchoring it into the rock. It seems like it grew there naturally, like the algae and barnacles, as if it was planted. The shack has survived raging storms, a fire, the biggest winter swells in memory, and thousands upon thousands of perfectly sunny days. It is a monument to the pioneers who have surfed, partied and died there, since Woody Brown first paddled out on a handmade, solid-wood board in 1937. It's often used for small weddings, christenings and funerals. It is a shrine, a temple, and a church, all in one. No wonder it was designated as a historical treasure in 1998.

Woody Ekstrom was fourteen when he jumped on his first surfboard in 1941.

At 93, Woody remembered helping his pals build the shack as if were only a few years ago. "I surfed for about 80 years!" He claims to have a photo of cows on the beach. Back then, he was a guy clutching a massive redwood plank surfboard. There were no wetsuits, leashes or Sticky Bumps Surf Wax. Until most of his friends returned from fighting in World War ll, he often surfed alone. Woody's younger brother, Carl, became a world-renowned board shaper.

Behind the shack is a steep incline that leads up to narrow strip of parking spots. In front of the parked cars, Glenn, a gray bearded artist, and WindanSea historian, sits on a 2 foot wide, flat rock wall, offering his paintings for sale. He takes a swig from a brown bottle of beer then curls up for his mid-morning nap. Pinned to the top corner of his painter's easel is a tiny American flag that snaps in the wind.

On the other side of the street, the local neighborhood meanders with an eclectic blend of tidy multi-million dollar homes. Tall, skinny palm trees line the streets, providing little shade. They sway and bend as if being wooed by the siren of the surf, straining

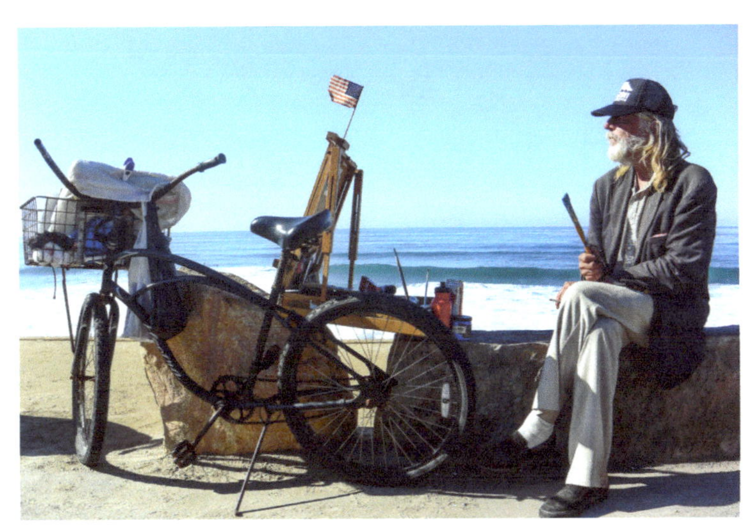

Glenn

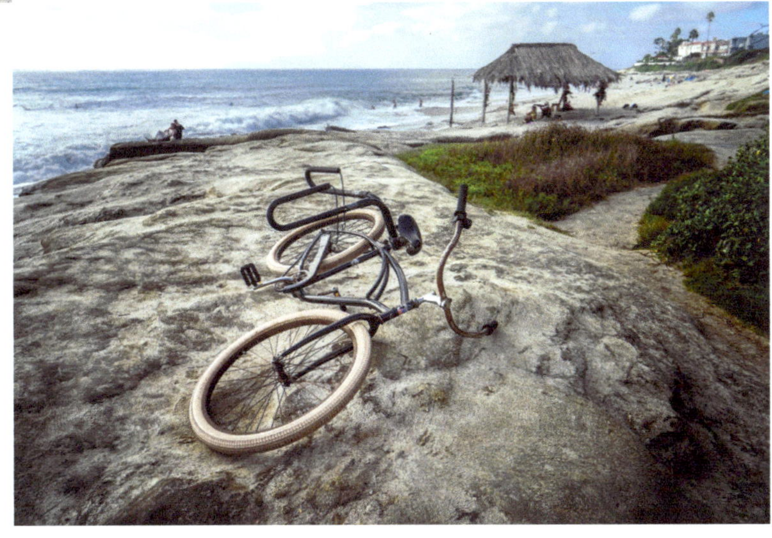

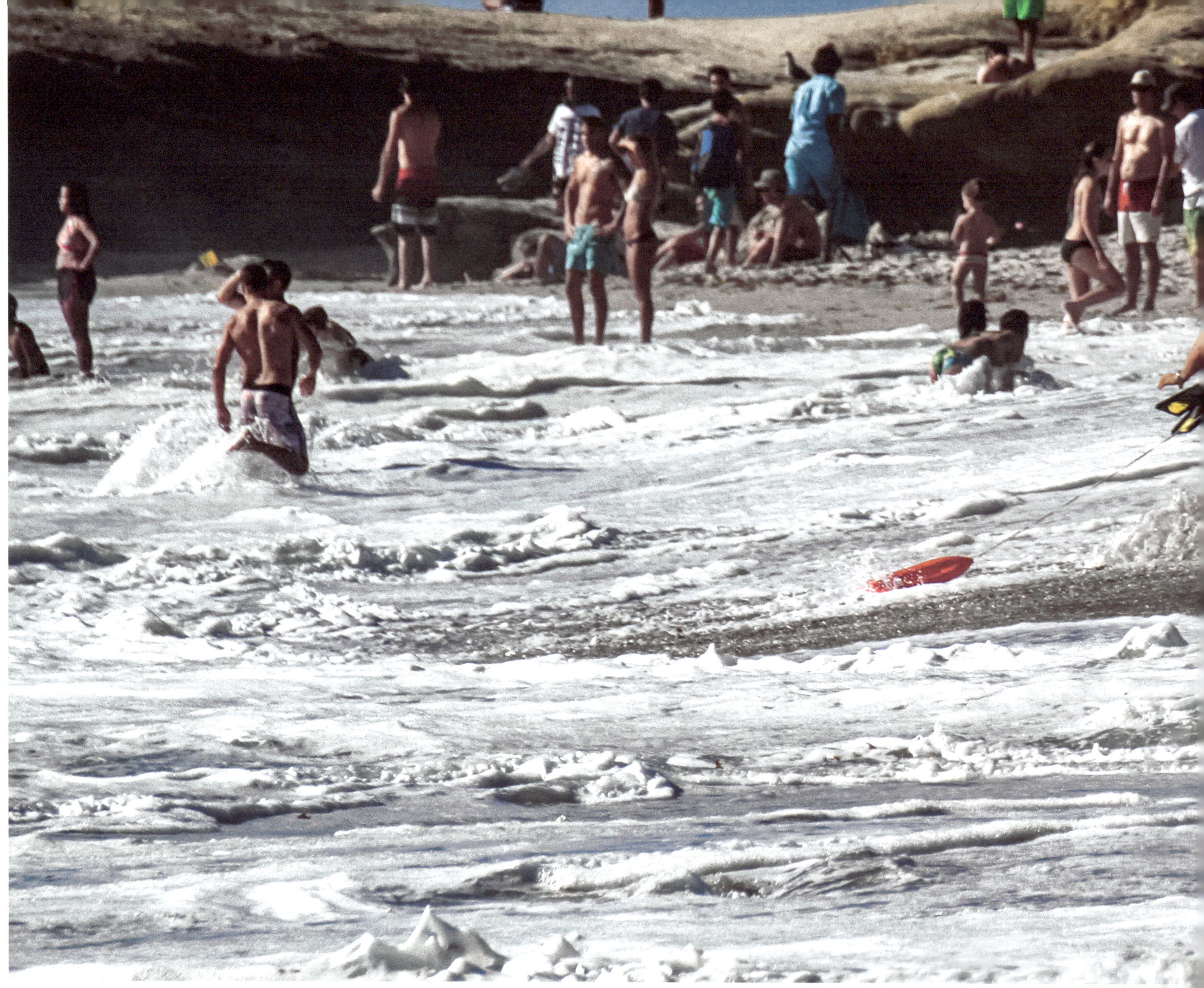

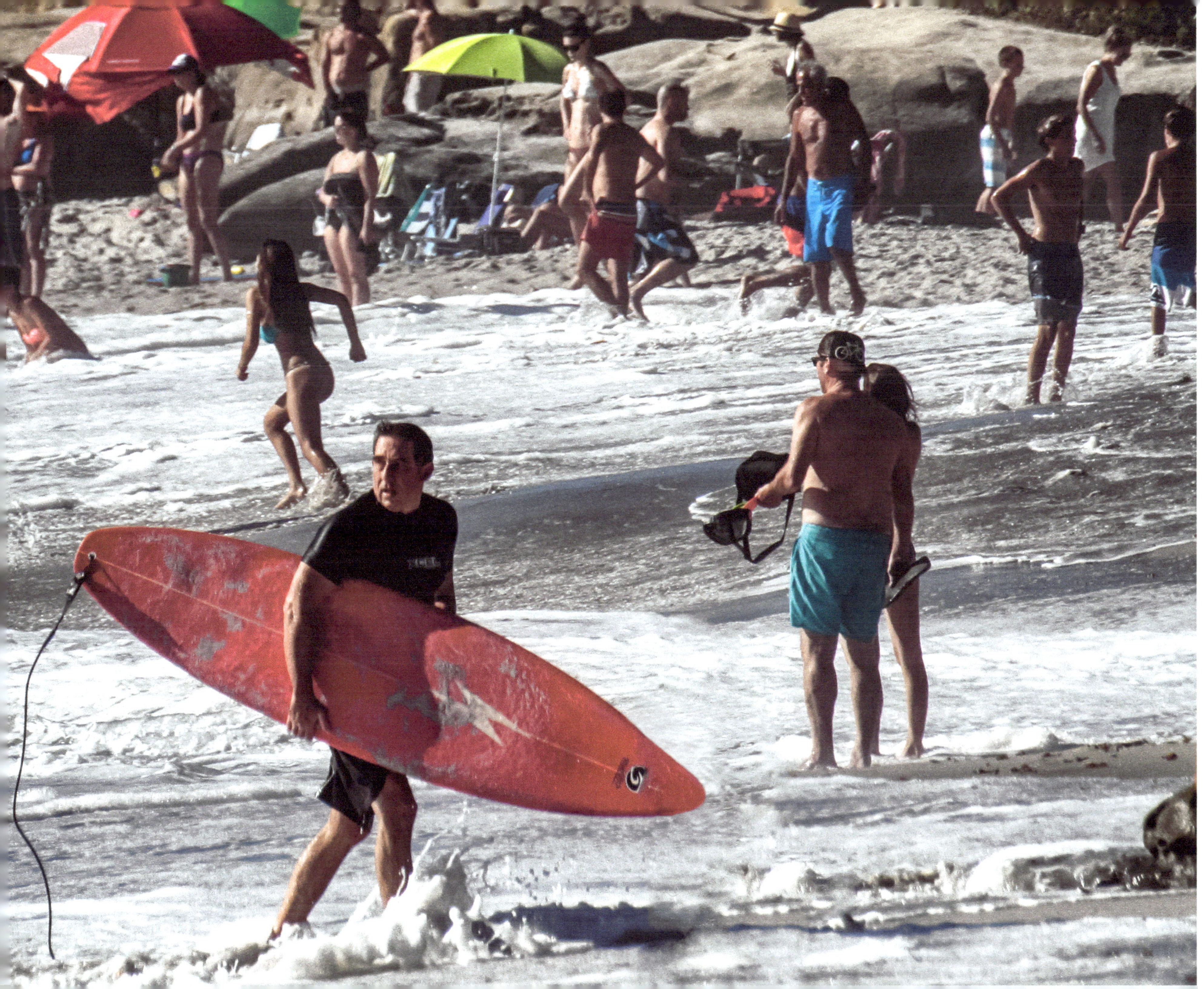

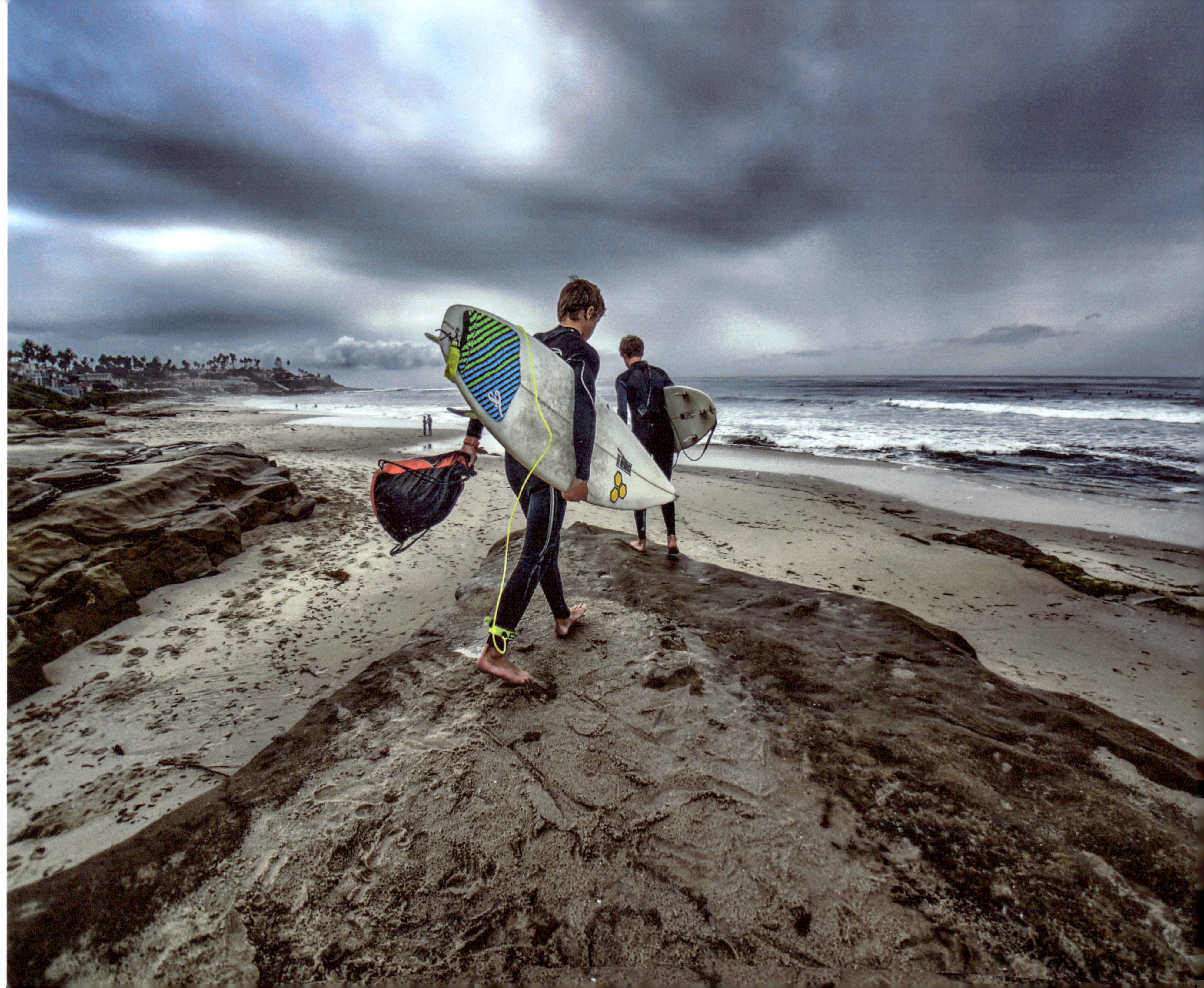

to size up the heavy waves rolling in. There is only one season this far south in La-La Land: the season of Beach, bathed in the warm breeze of affluence and life-is-easy.

Just off shore, grows a tangled bed of kelp shading a reef, with deep water channels plunging down around it; all working together to help form near perfect waves that peel both left and right.

As the surfing culture mushroomed, those who didn't have access to a beach could always find some smooth pavement. *Sidewalk surfing*—skateboarding—took hold and eventually branched to snowboarding. Surf music provided another long-lasting component to the emerging lifestyle. Dick Dale and the Del-Tones, Jan & Dean, The Ventures and The Beach Boys gave us earworm-y guitar solos and riffs, many becoming the soundtracks of our lives.

Surf slang provided important code words to let your friends know that you belonged to (or wanted to belong to) the surfing tribe: *stoked* (happy), *groovy* (good), *bitchin'*

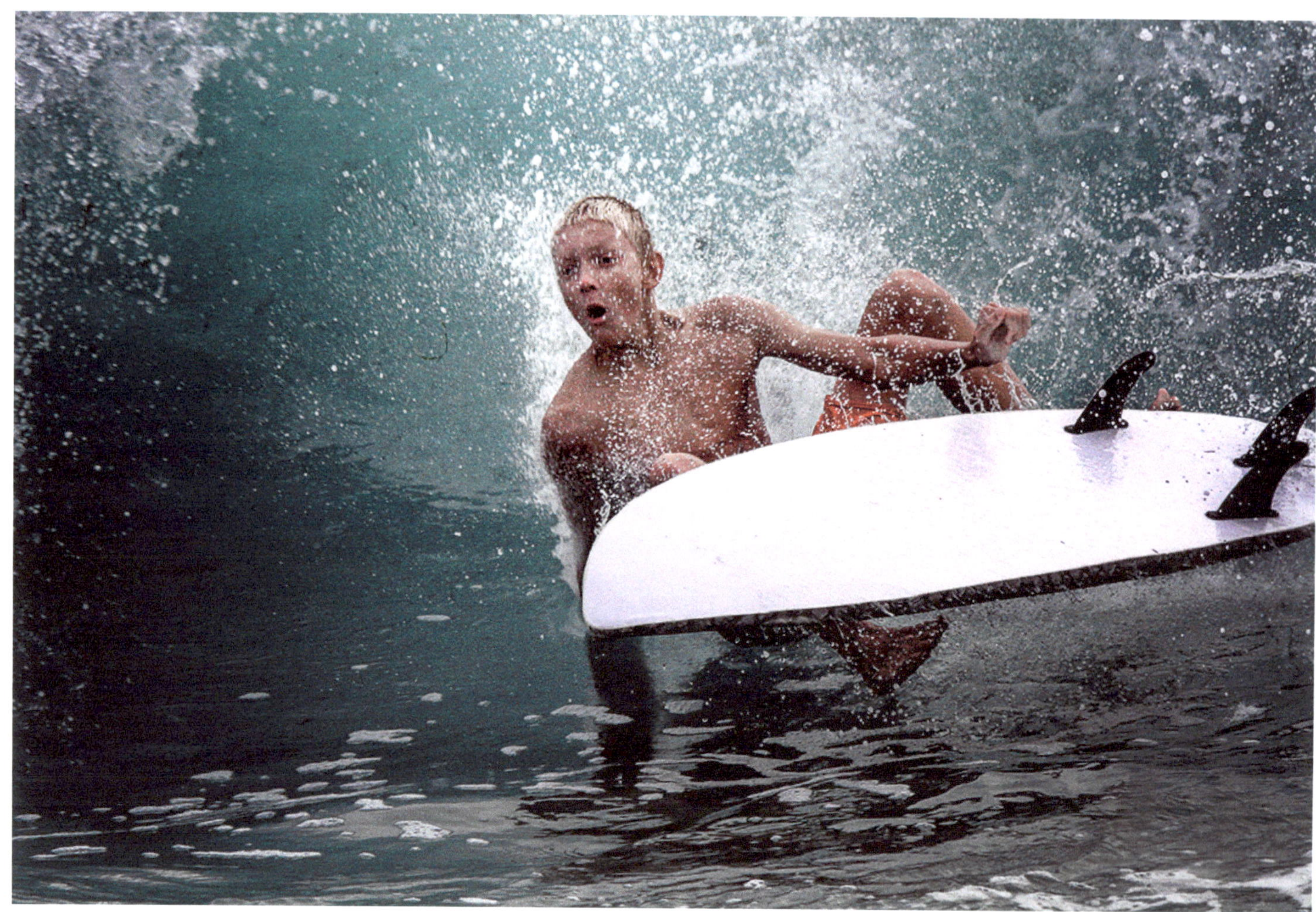

Wiping out is an underappreciated skill.

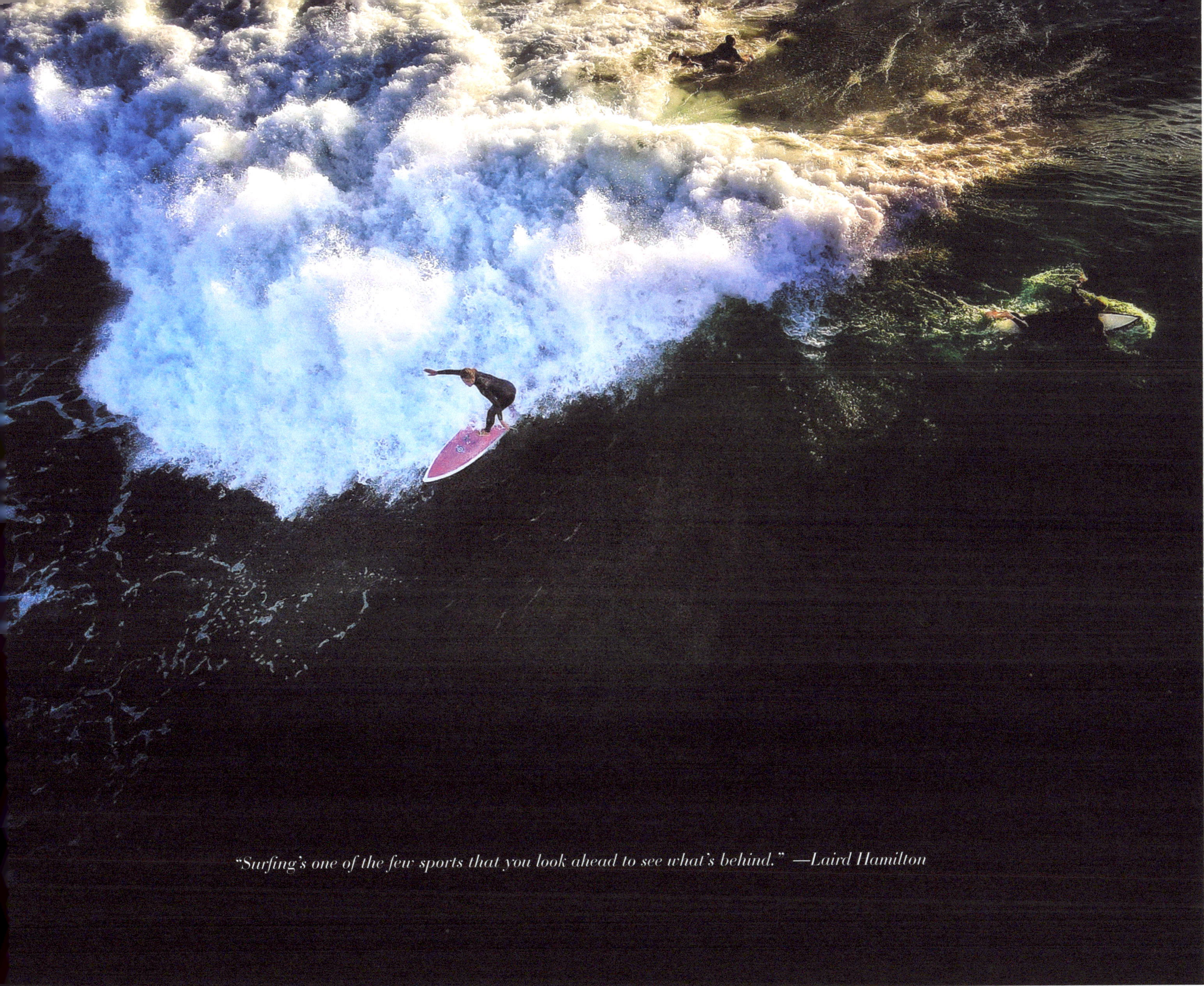

"Surfing's one of the few sports that you look ahead to see what's behind." —Laird Hamilton

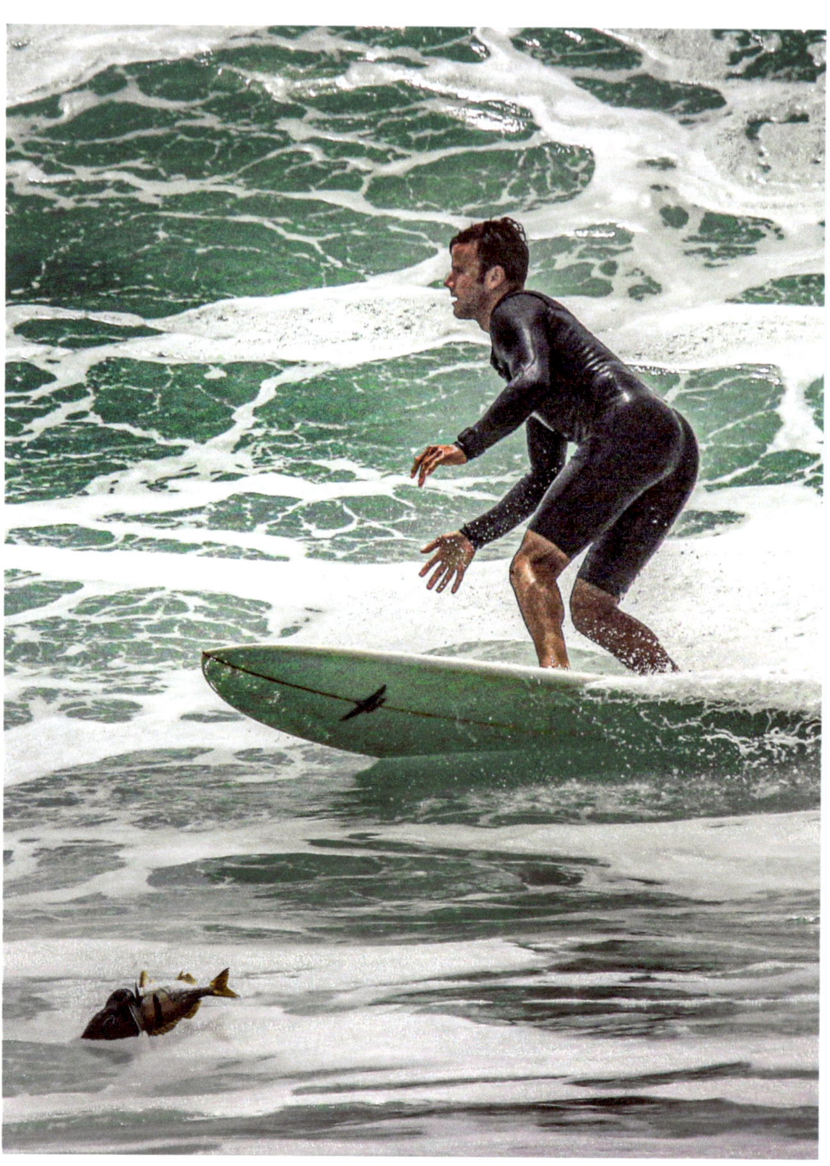

Seal enjoying a meal with a view.

16

(really good), *cowabunga* (cried out enthusiastically when surfing), *brah* (fellow surfer), *gnarly* (dangerous surf conditions), *eat it* (wiping out), *landlord* (shark), *grom* (a young surfer), *frube* (a surfer who doesn't catch a wave the entire time they're in the water).

From The Beach Boys "Surfin' USA"

If everybody had an ocean
Across the USA
Then everybody'd be surfin'
Like Californi-a
You'd seen them wearing their baggies
Huarache sandals too
A bushy blond hairdo
Surfin' USA

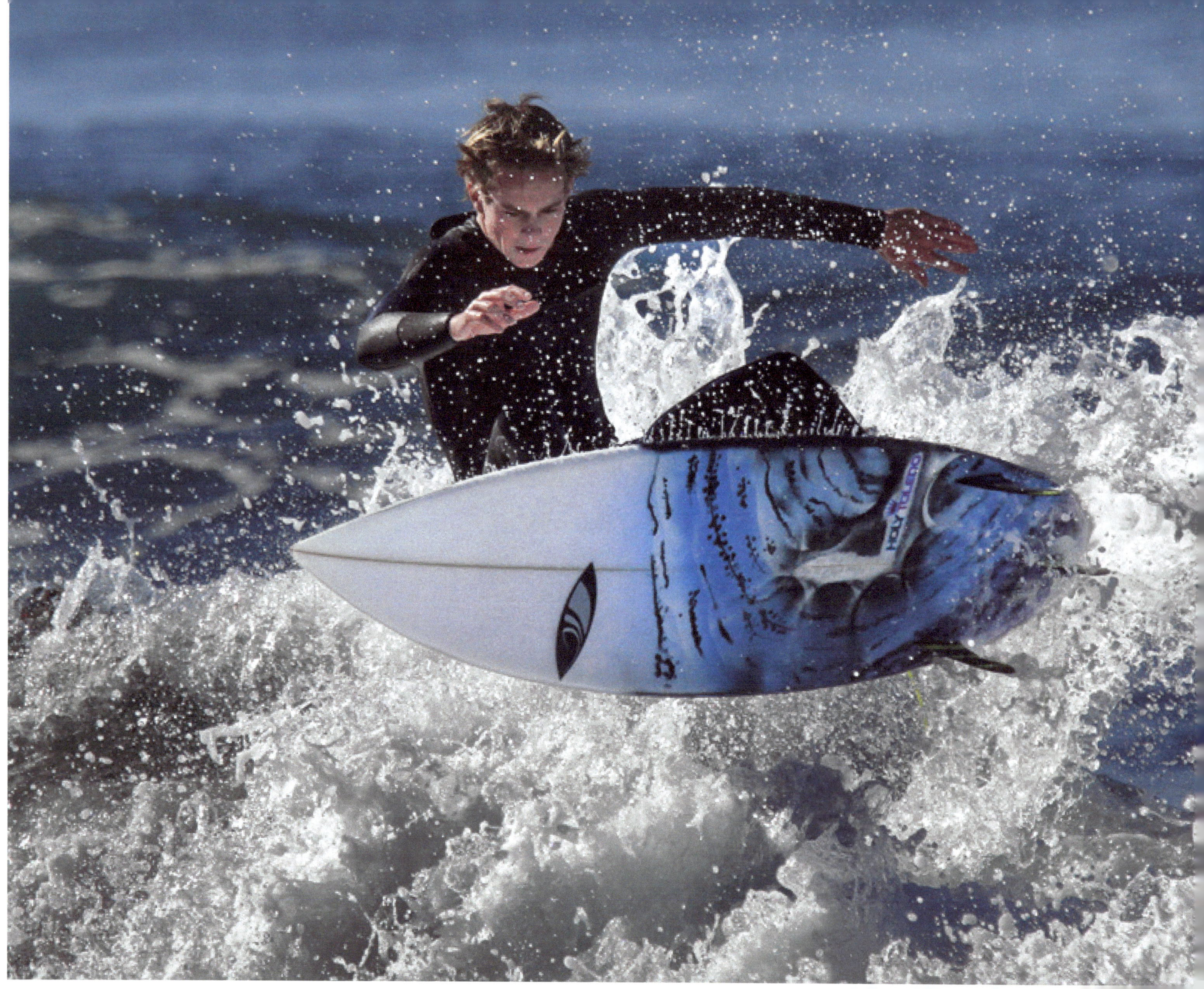

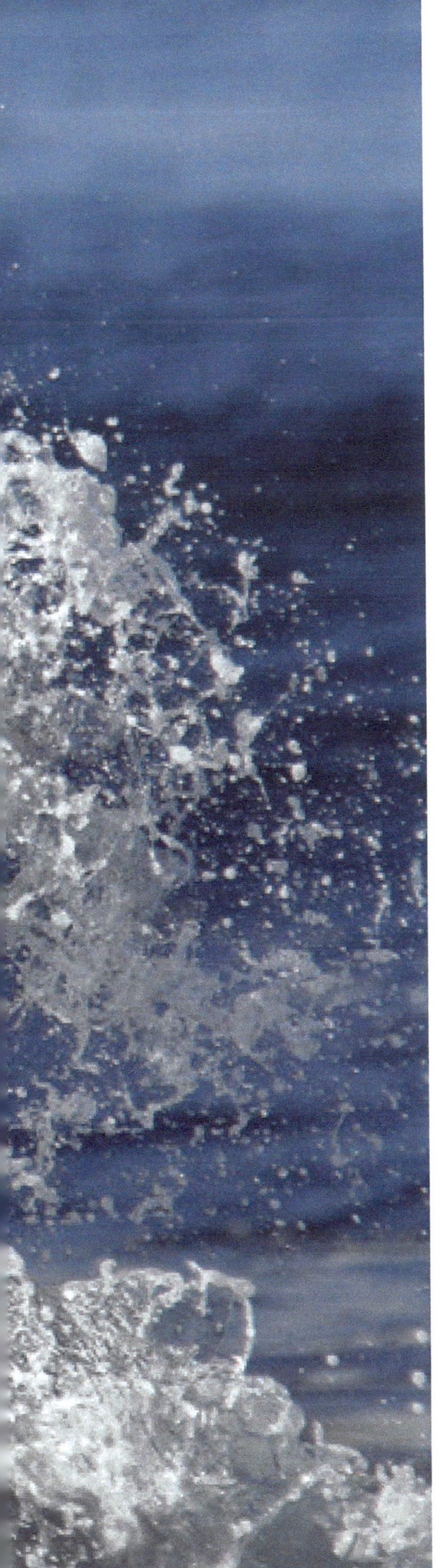

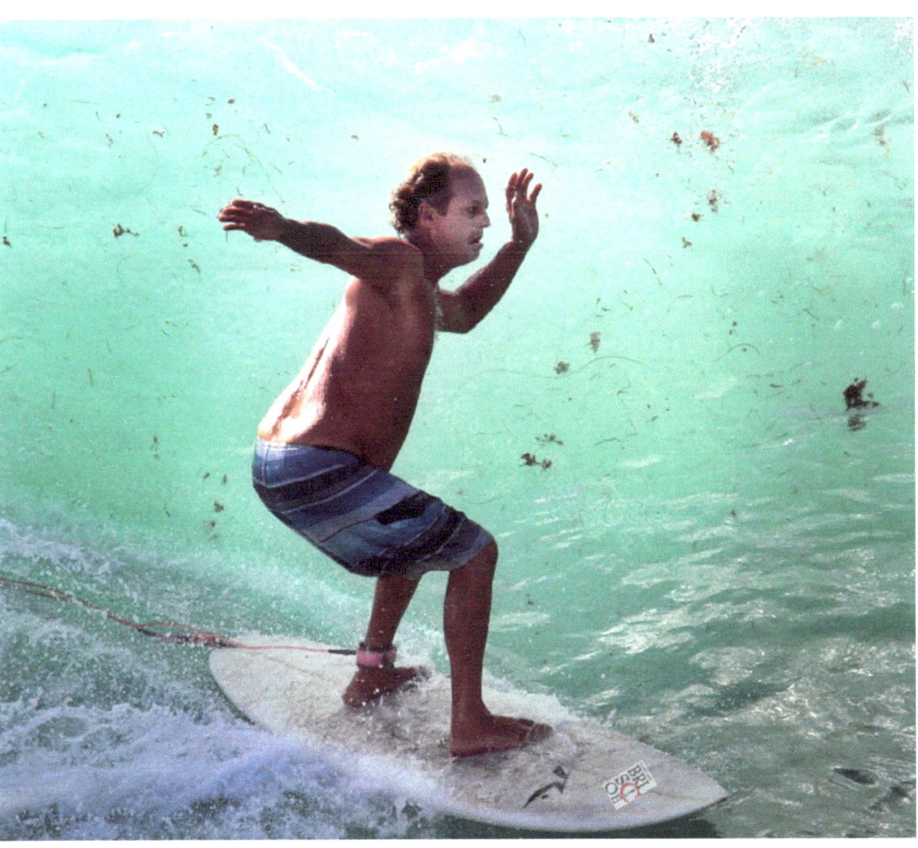

There are a million ways to surf, and as long as you're having fun, you're doing it right.

Beneath the pristine wrapping of this beautiful place is a history of surf lore that reads more like the Wild West than Pleasantville. Steve Pezman, a publisher of *Surfer* and of *The Surfer's Journal*, called WindanSea locals in the early 1960s, "the heaviest surf crew ever." During that decade of peace and love, teams of San Diego police were often called in to break up beach parties of nearly 500 strong. In late 1962, Northern Division Police Captain Howard Charman, now retired, met with Senior Lifeguard Bill Cosgrove and Aquatic Superintendent Don Venne to plan a crackdown on the rowdy surfers.

"…boy, you better straighten up and fly right."

"WindanSea got to be a real pain in the butt." Charman said. "Citizens around there were getting uptight, and justifiably so. Broken beer bottles, litter, surfers going up into people's yards and peeing all over the place. First we warned them, 'If you're going to surf WindanSea Beach, boy, you better straighten up and fly right.'

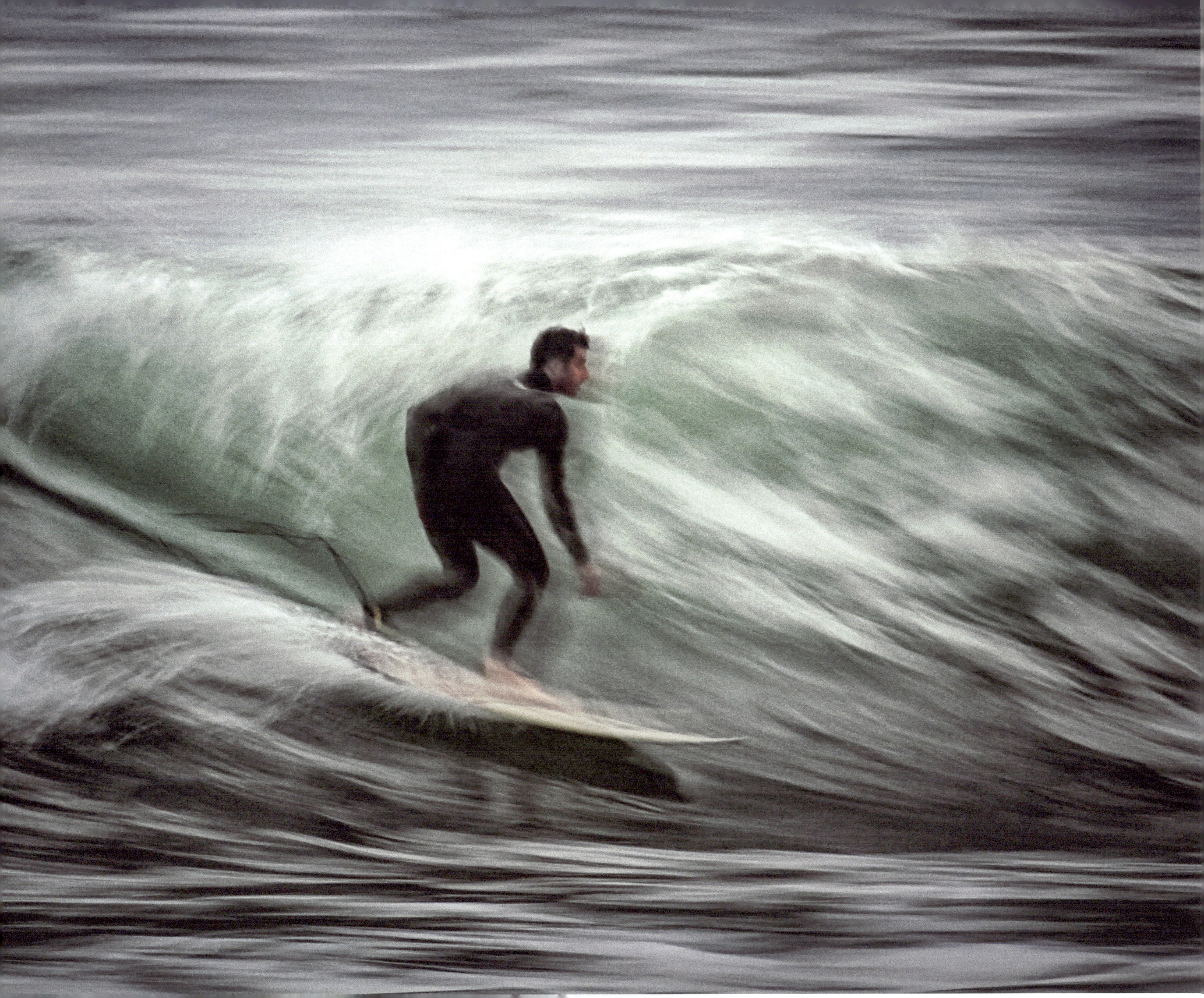

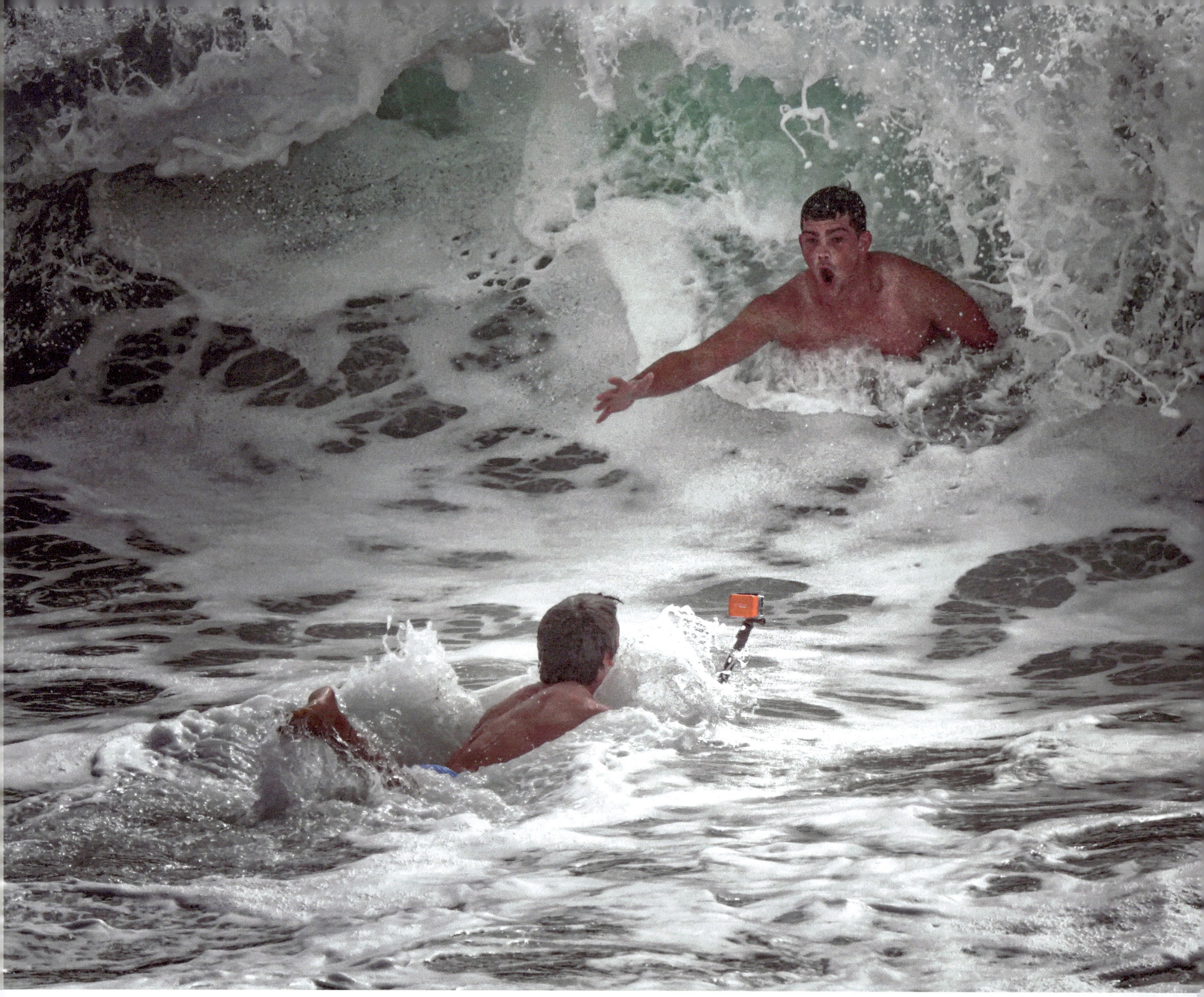

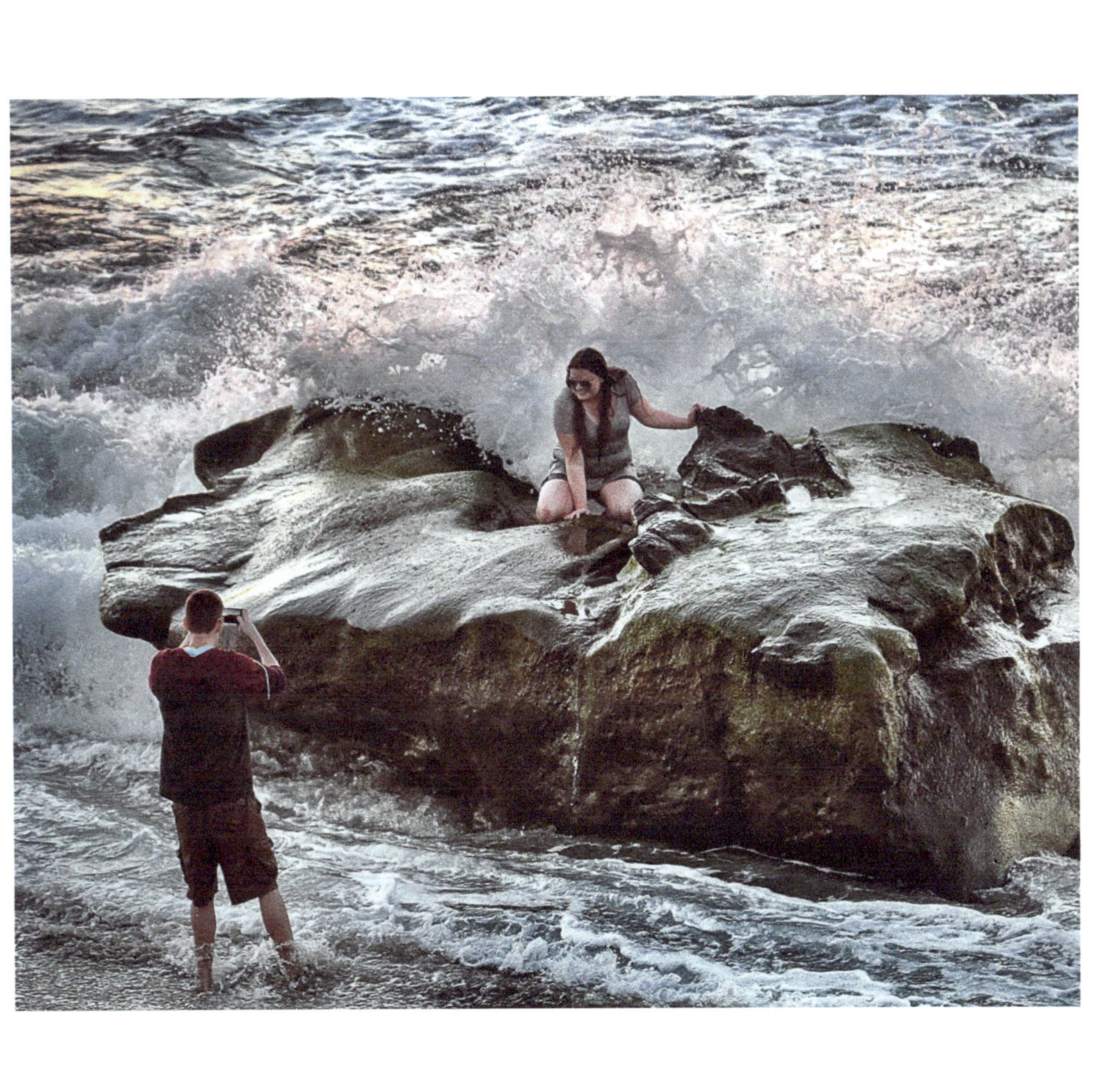

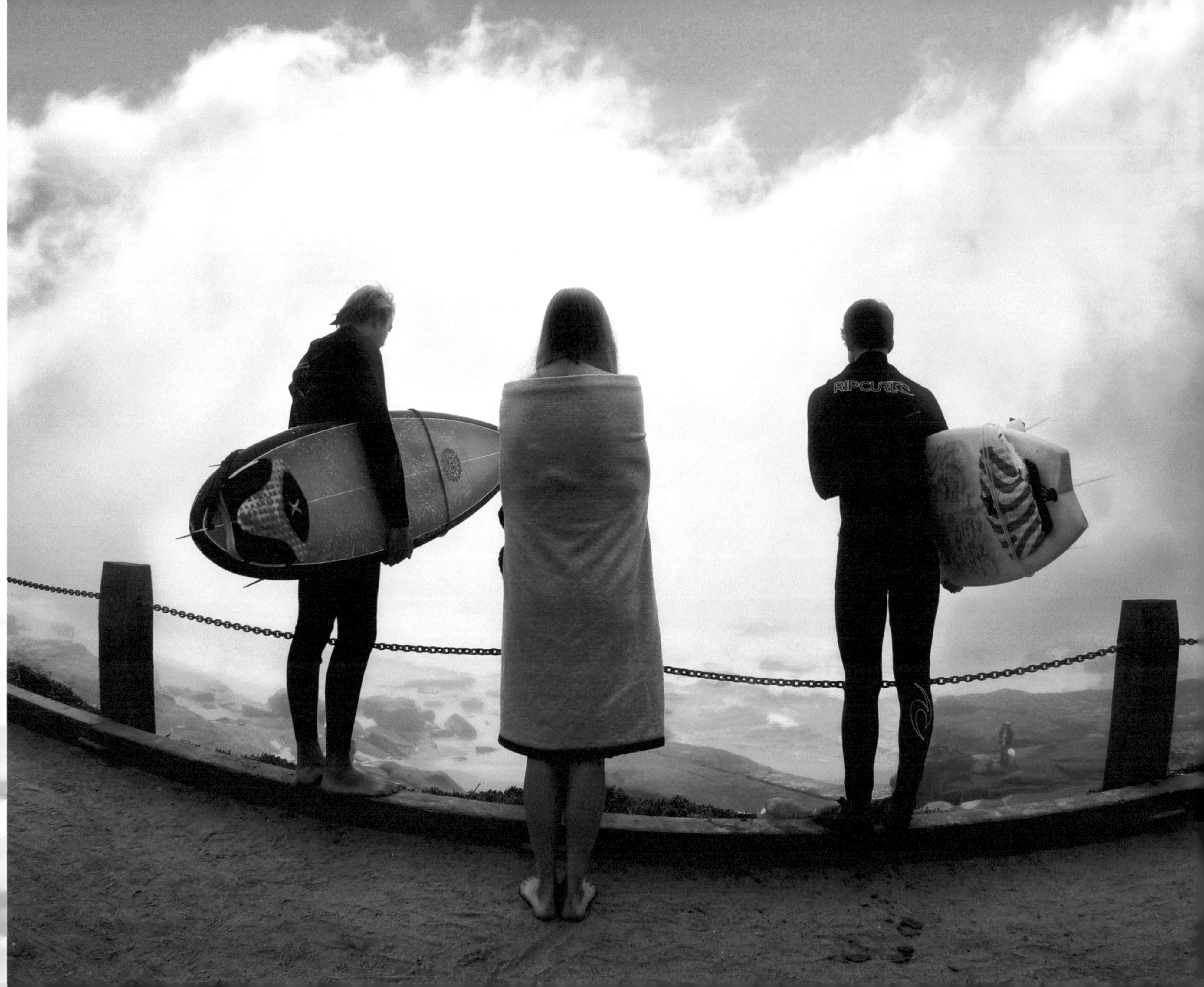

Then we put the pressure on. We had more tickets than they had money and we were very generous with them [the tickets]. We warned the surfers we could pass an ordinance to prohibit surfing at WindanSea."

They had hijacked a pie truck...

Surfer and filmmaker, Greg Noll once offered, "It was as if someone moved Bellevue Psychiatric Hospital to the beach and turned the inmates loose at WindanSea. I remember filming there and Tiny Brain Thomas was getting rolled down the cliff in a metal trashcan. Then there was this huge pie fight. They had hijacked a pie truck, wiped it out and the next thing you know there was like 20 guys slinging pies at each other....They were the worst fuck-ups on the coast, absolutely no question about it."

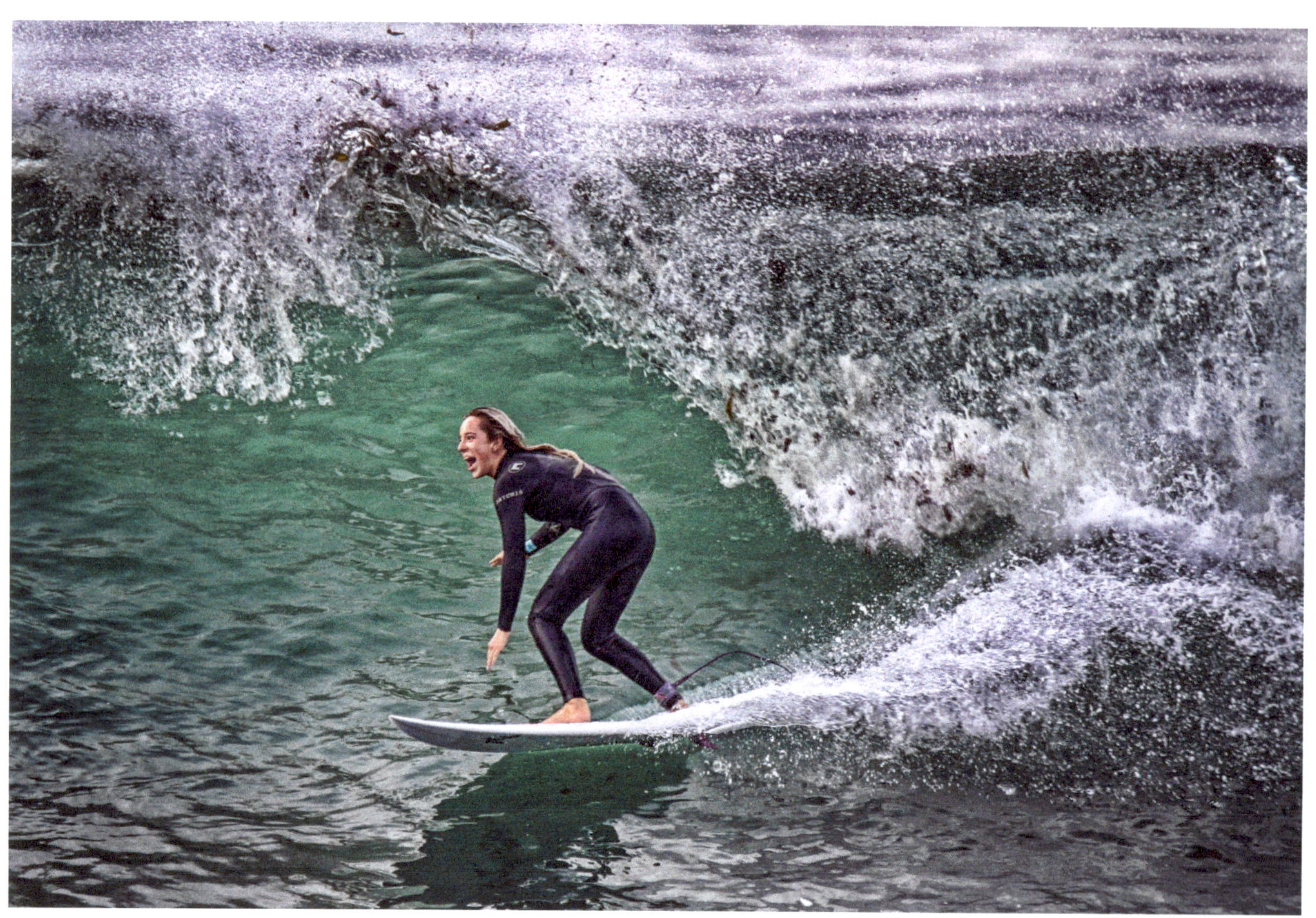

Getting a dose of vitamin sea.

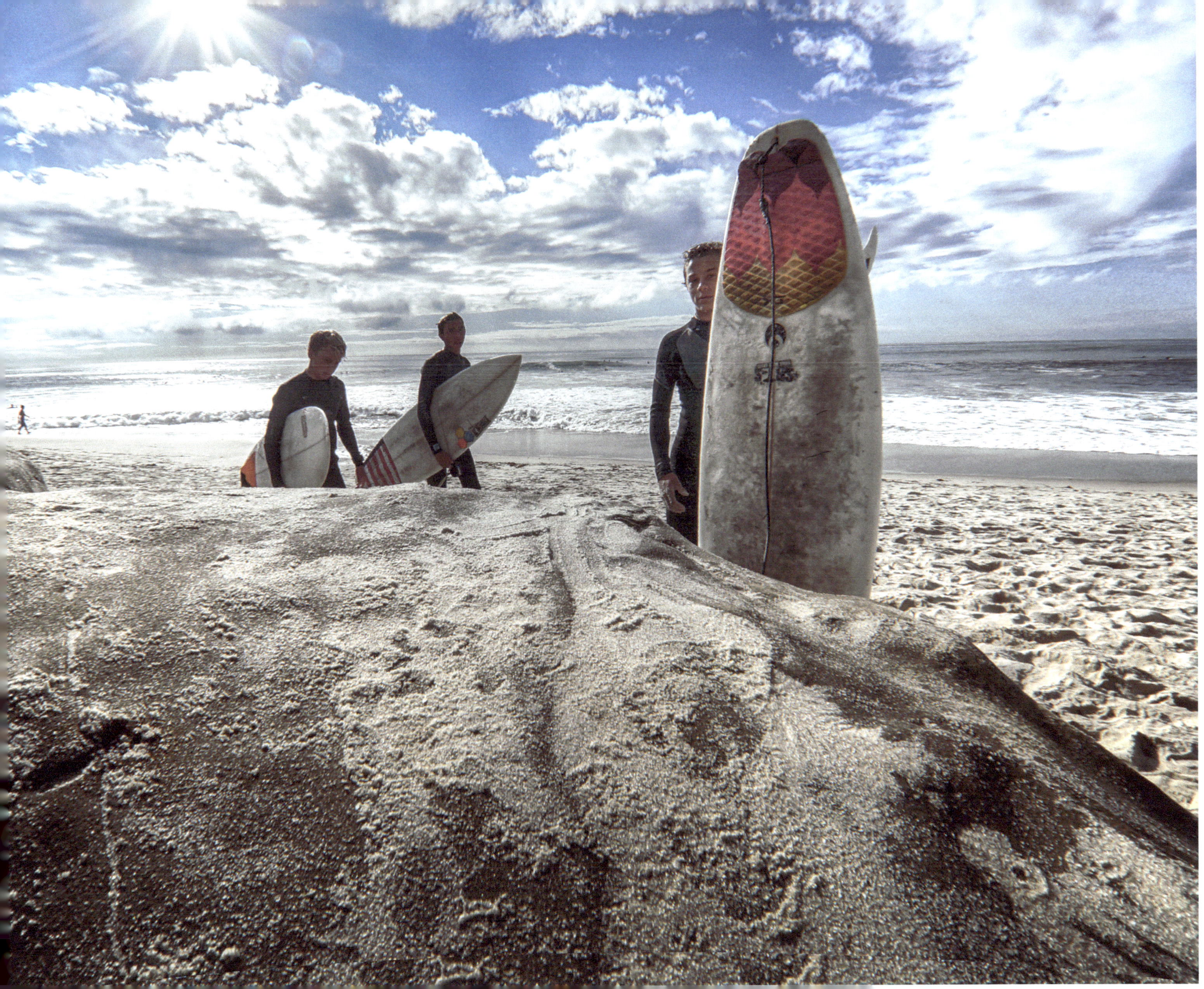

Not too long ago on a tribute Facebook page remembering the-out-of-control antics of WindanSea surfer, Butch Van Artsdalen, fellow wave rider Dick Mobley wrote, "We were going up to John Petit's house to get something to eat once. Billy Graham sees us driving away and says 'Where ya going?' and we tell him where. 'Bring me back a sandwich!' 'OK!' So we drove up and made him a shit sandwich. I don't remember who or what supplied that shit, but we put it in the bread with lettuce, mayo and everything. It looked great. We bring it down to Graham and hand it to him through the car window.

"...his eyes start to bug out..."

He takes the sandwich, unwraps it and opens his mouth for a big bite. Suddenly his upper lip begins to curl and his eyes start to bug out as he realizes what he's about to bite into. We were already starting to drive away at this point. Graham was about the toughest guy at WindanSea and we knew we had better get out of there fast."

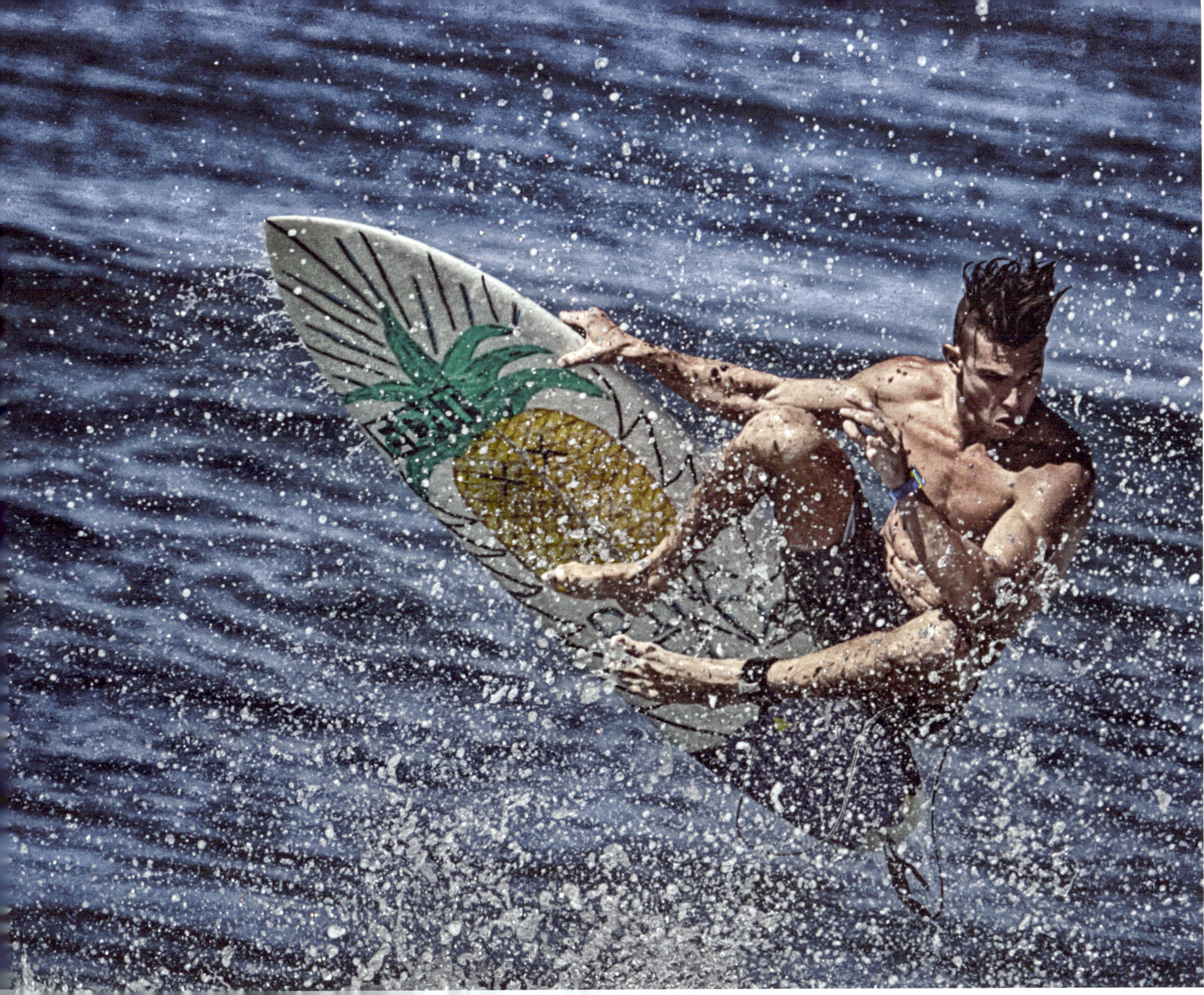

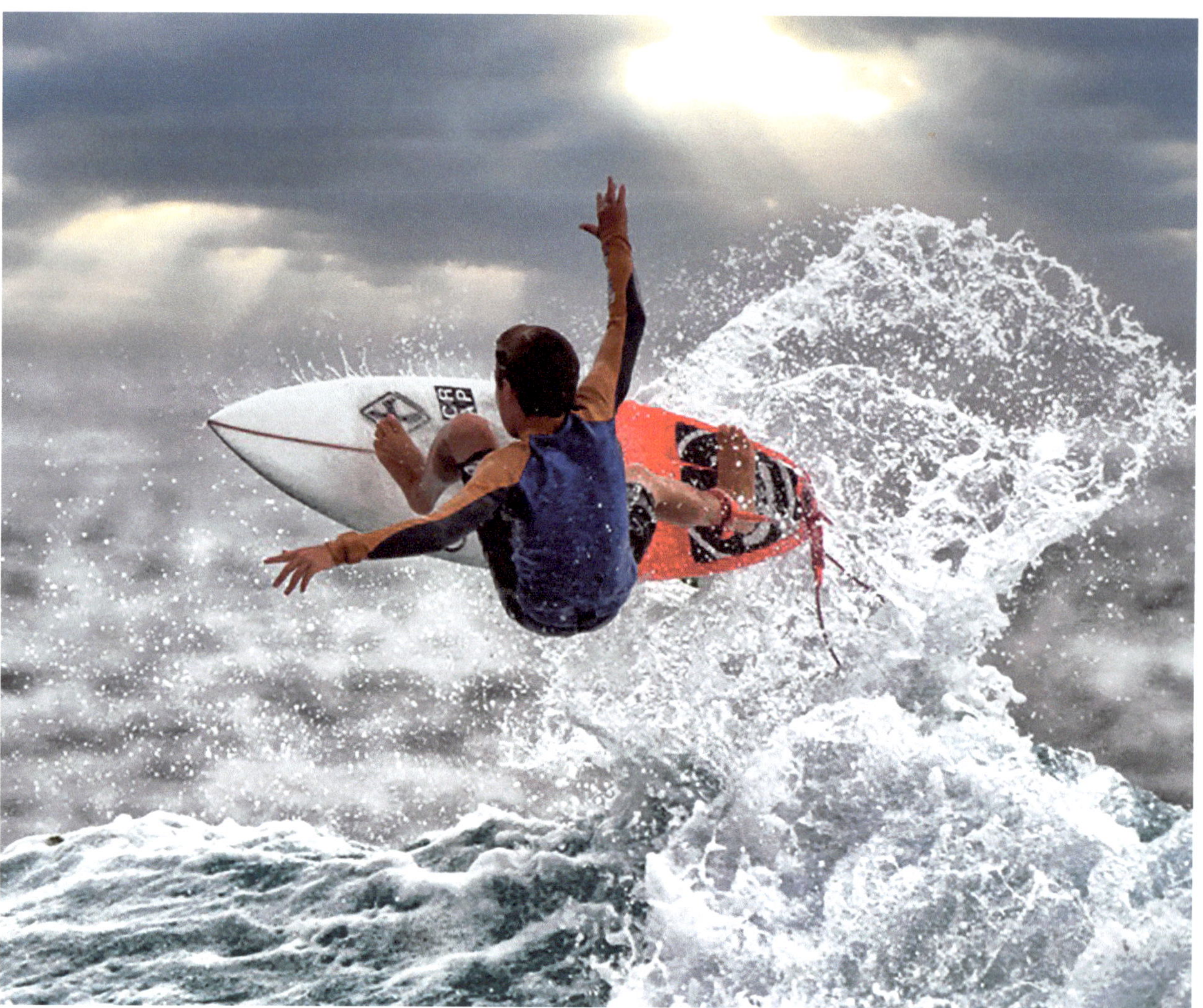

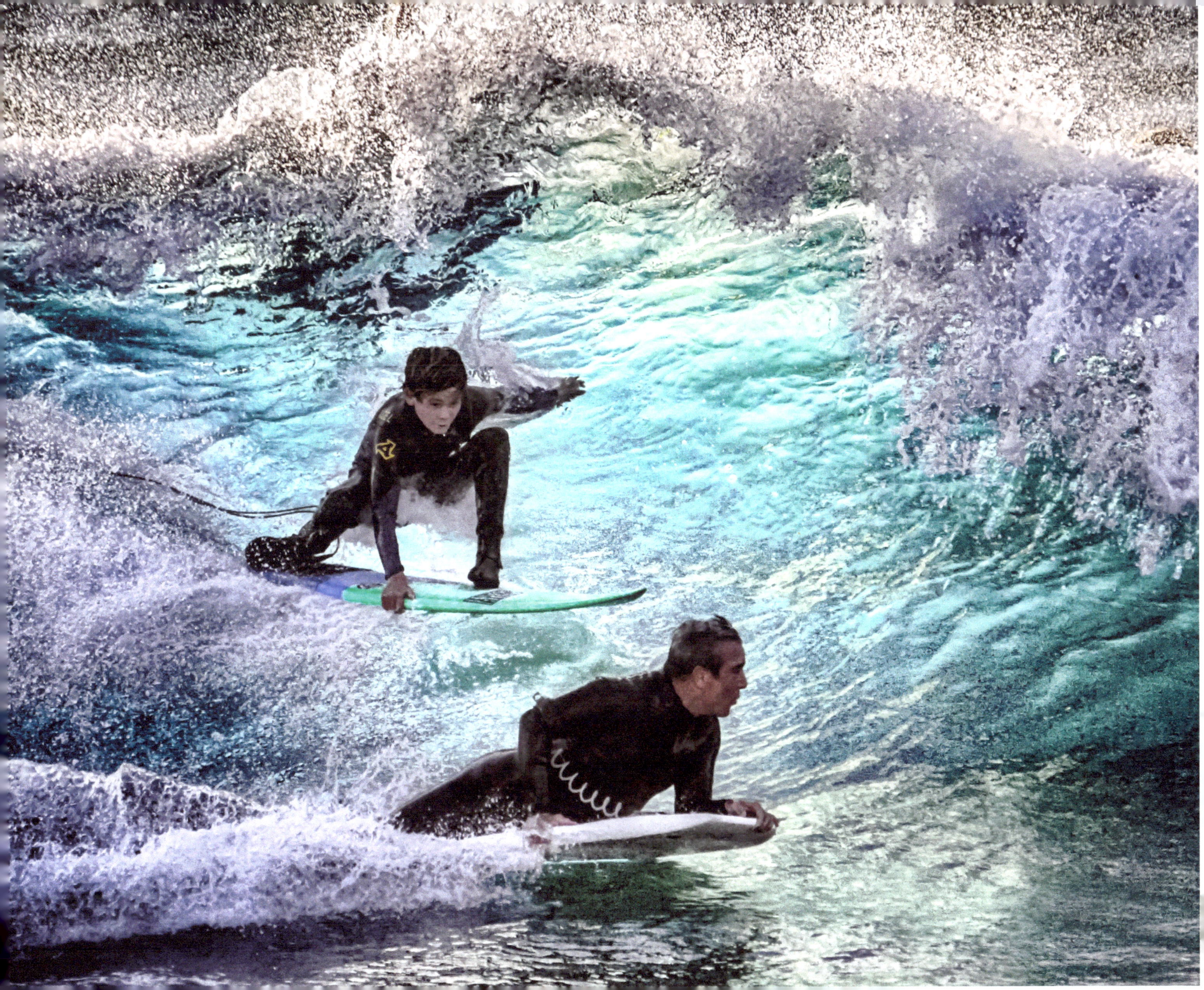

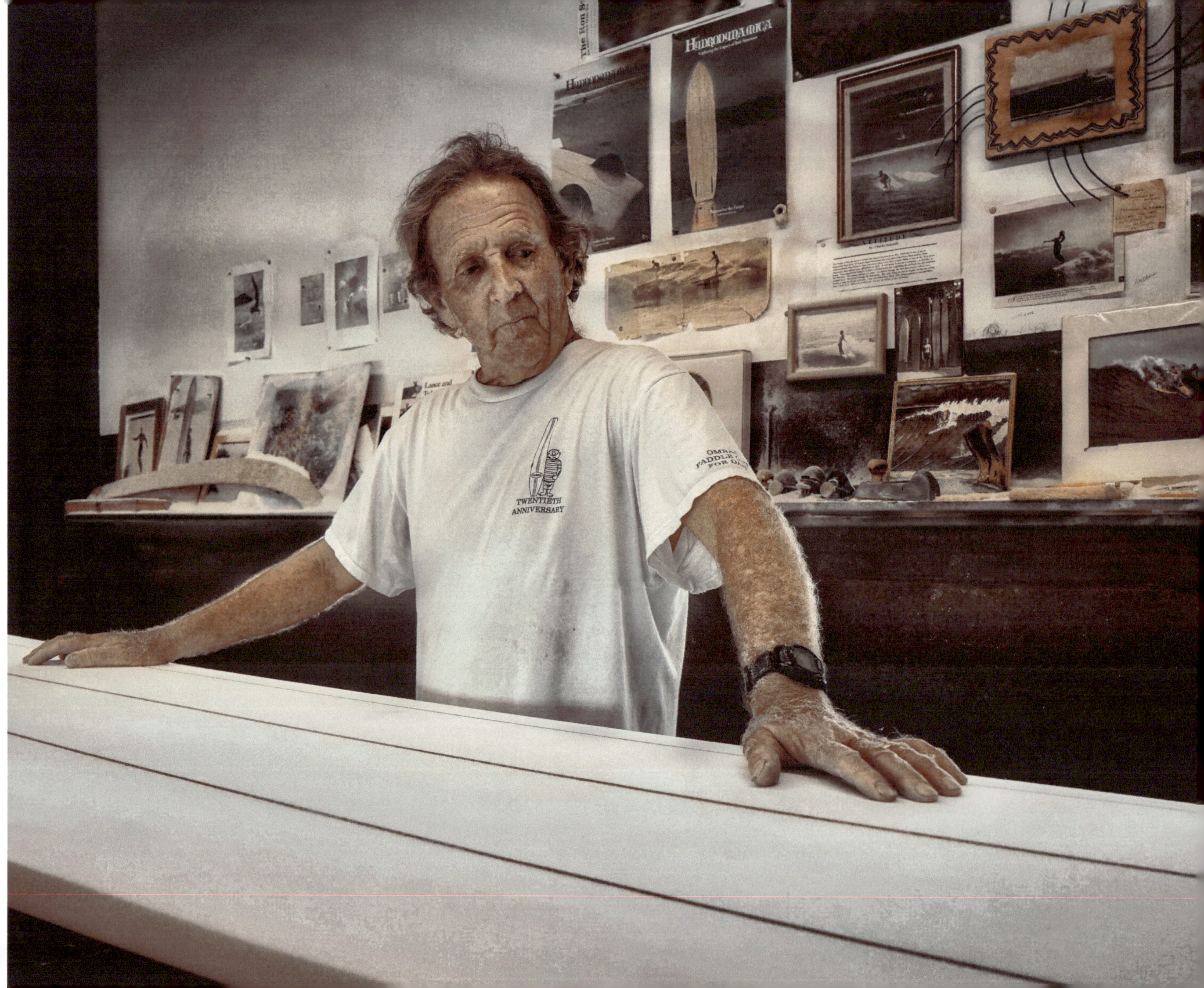

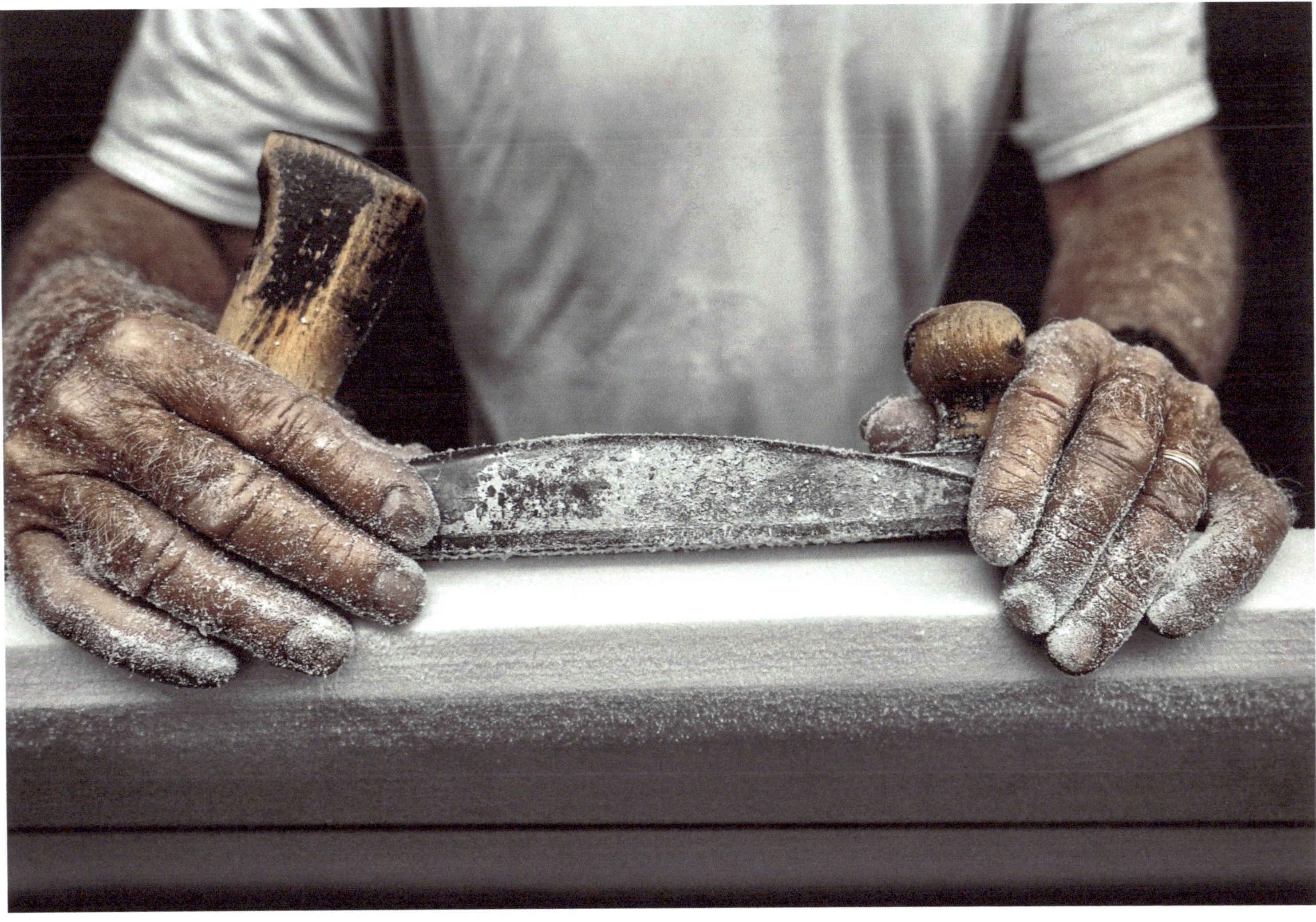

Skip Frye began surfing in 1958. About five years later, he began shaping boards. Skip has traveled the world, successfully competing as a surfer and featured on various surf magazine covers. Aaron Pai, founder of the Surfers' Hall of Fame said, "Skip Frye is one of the all-time great surfers and one of the all-time great surfboard shapers! Skip is true surfing royalty," Many would say that surfboard design in the USA progressed largely because of Skip's innovations. He once remarked, "Surfing to me is like playing music. You play different melodies with different boards." He still creates some of the most in-demand surfboards in the world—many are collector's pieces, passed down through generations. Skip surfs almost every day. You'll never see him wear a leash.

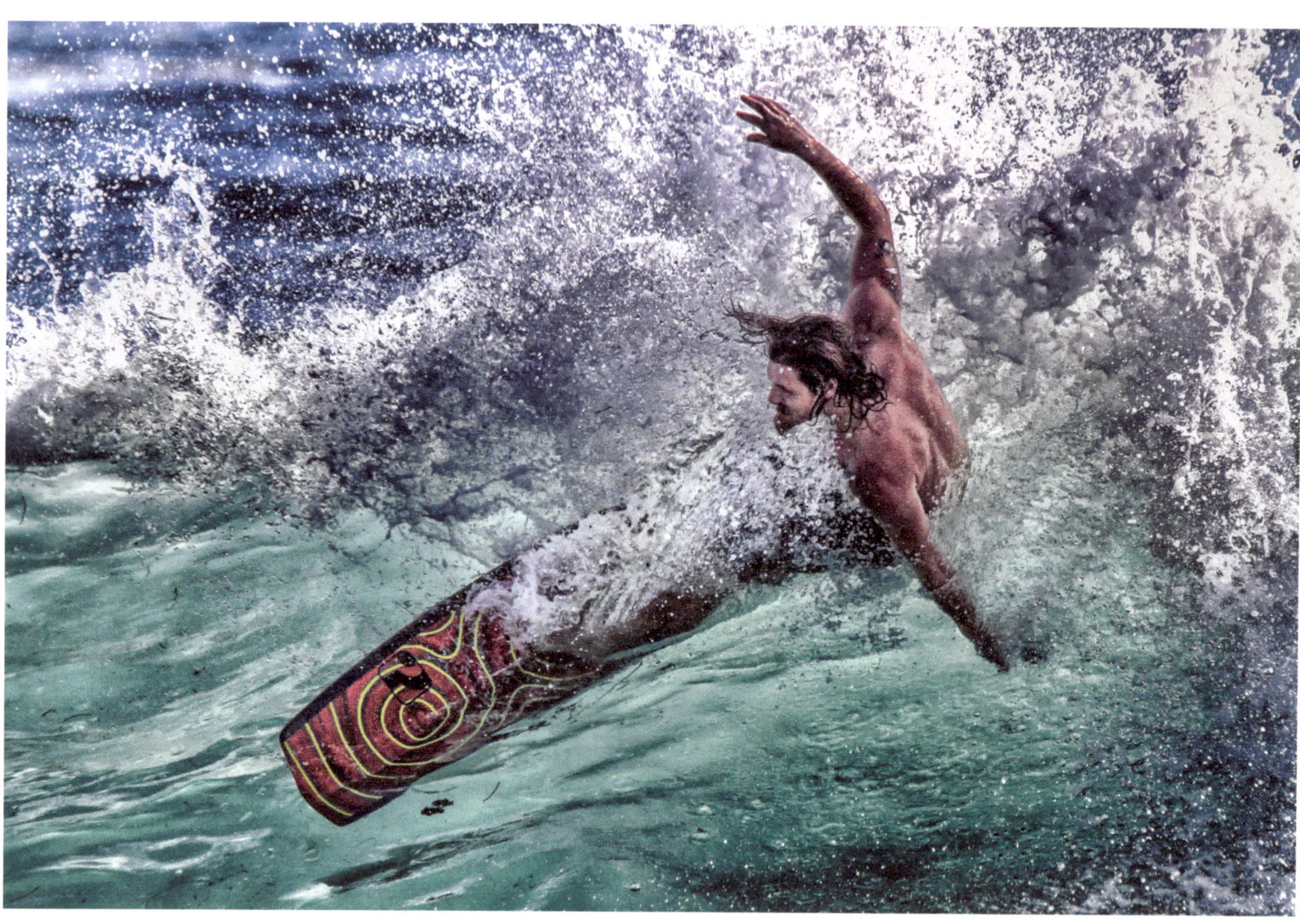

On the same FaceBook page, Billie Graham smacked back, "I threw that f**king thing at them as they sped off. I swear, if I would have bit into that sandwich there would have been death that day. I would have killed them both. But I'll take care of business. Mobley and Petit will never see it coming either. Time is on my side. Revenge will be sweet."

In another FaceBook post Graham recalled, "You couldn't relax your guard for one minute at WindanSea. The minute you did they got ya. One summer this craze with throwing eggs at each other got started. If you've ever been hit with an egg you know that it hurts like a bitch. You'd be walking along the sidewalk or crossing a street and a car would pull up. Next thing you knew a bunch of guys you knew would jump out and start nailing you with eggs. Or you would be driving your car and someone would pull up next to you at an intersection and PIFF! PIFF! PIFF! all over your windshield and hood.

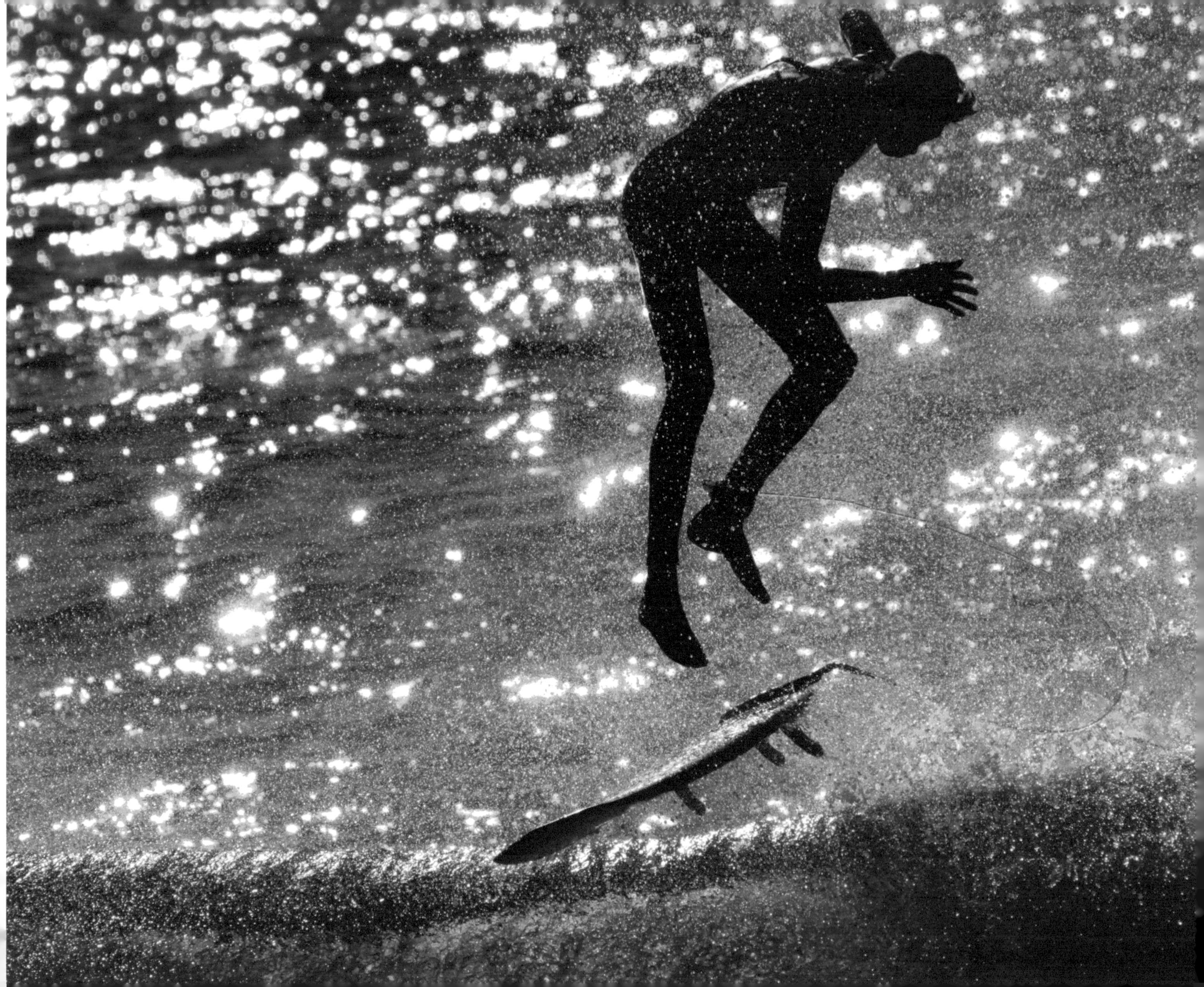

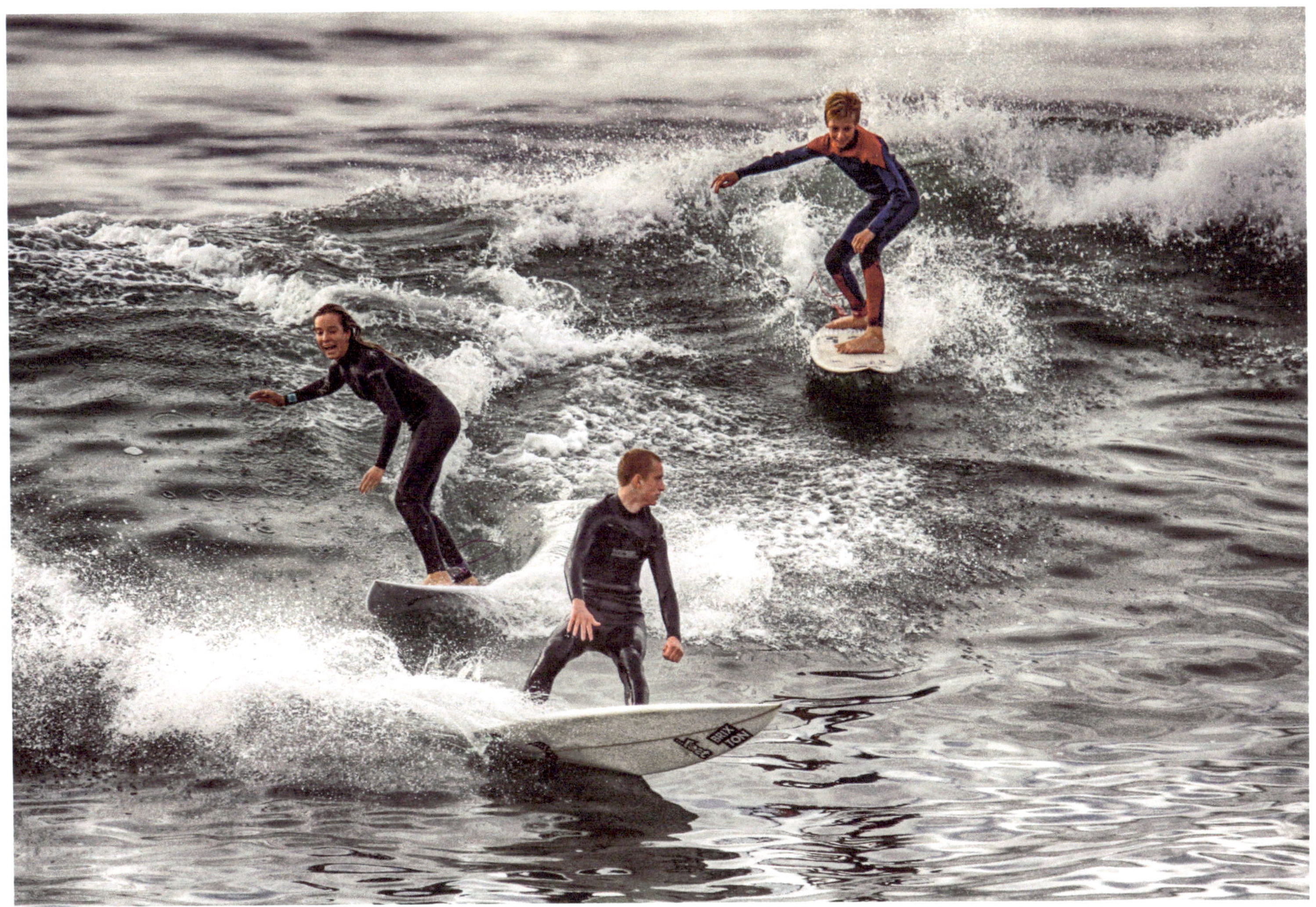

"I think we have to teach a lot to these kids—to first be gentlemen. Try to help one another and not hog the doggone waves." Duke Kahanamoku

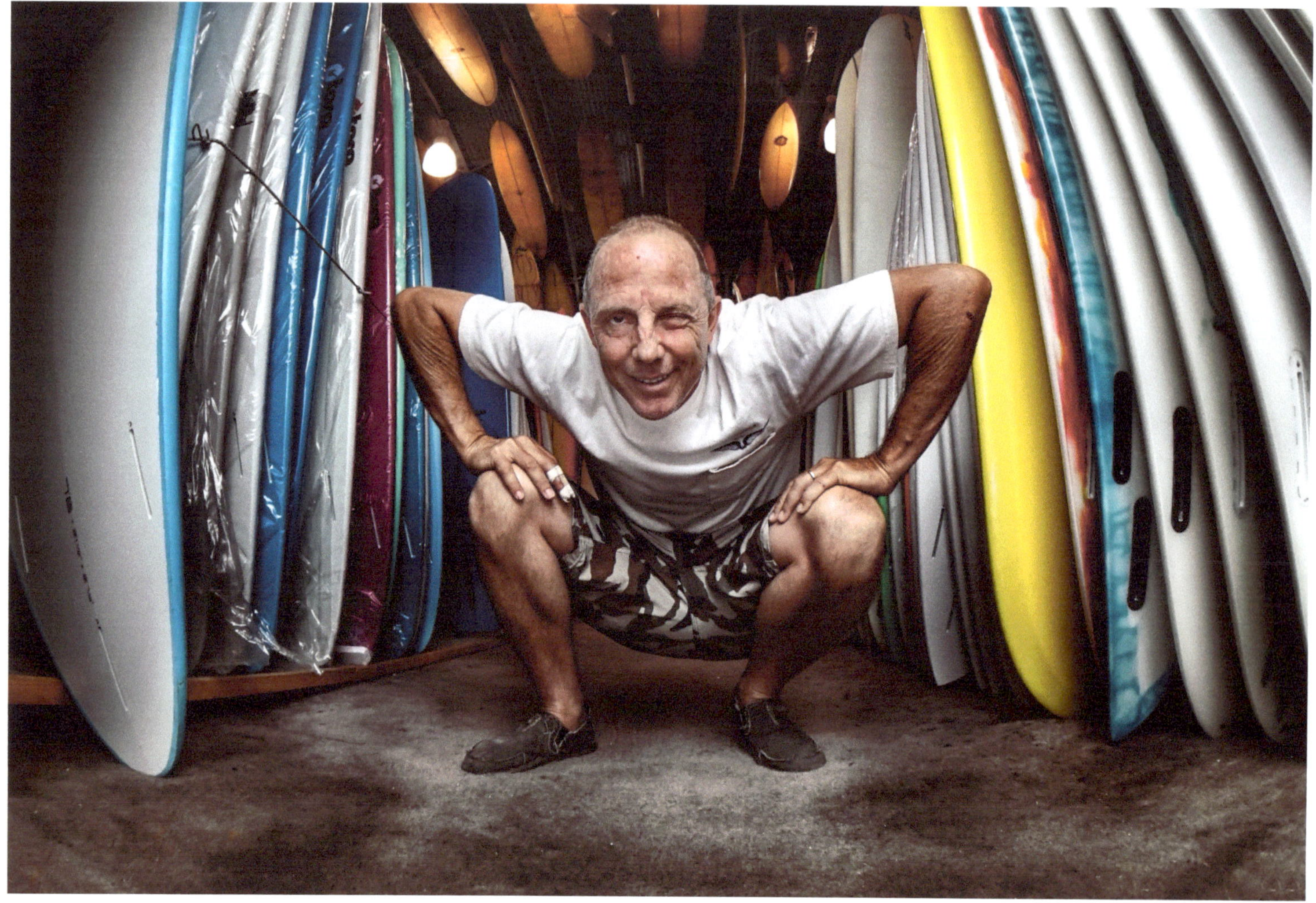

Bird, aka Eric Huffman, started to surf when he was a kid. "I don't think I'll ever lose my stoke for surfing. I think I'll do it until I can no longer breathe. It got inside of me and just won't go away." Bird has been doing surf reports on the radio, then online, since the '70s. In 2007 he opened Bird's Surf Shed, home to more than a thousand surfboards. He calls it his room of wonders—his library—boards that tell their own stories from the 1930s to the present time, paying homage to everyone who has made surfing what it is. "I like to get here early so I can listen to the boards talk… I've never met a surfboard that I haven't liked."

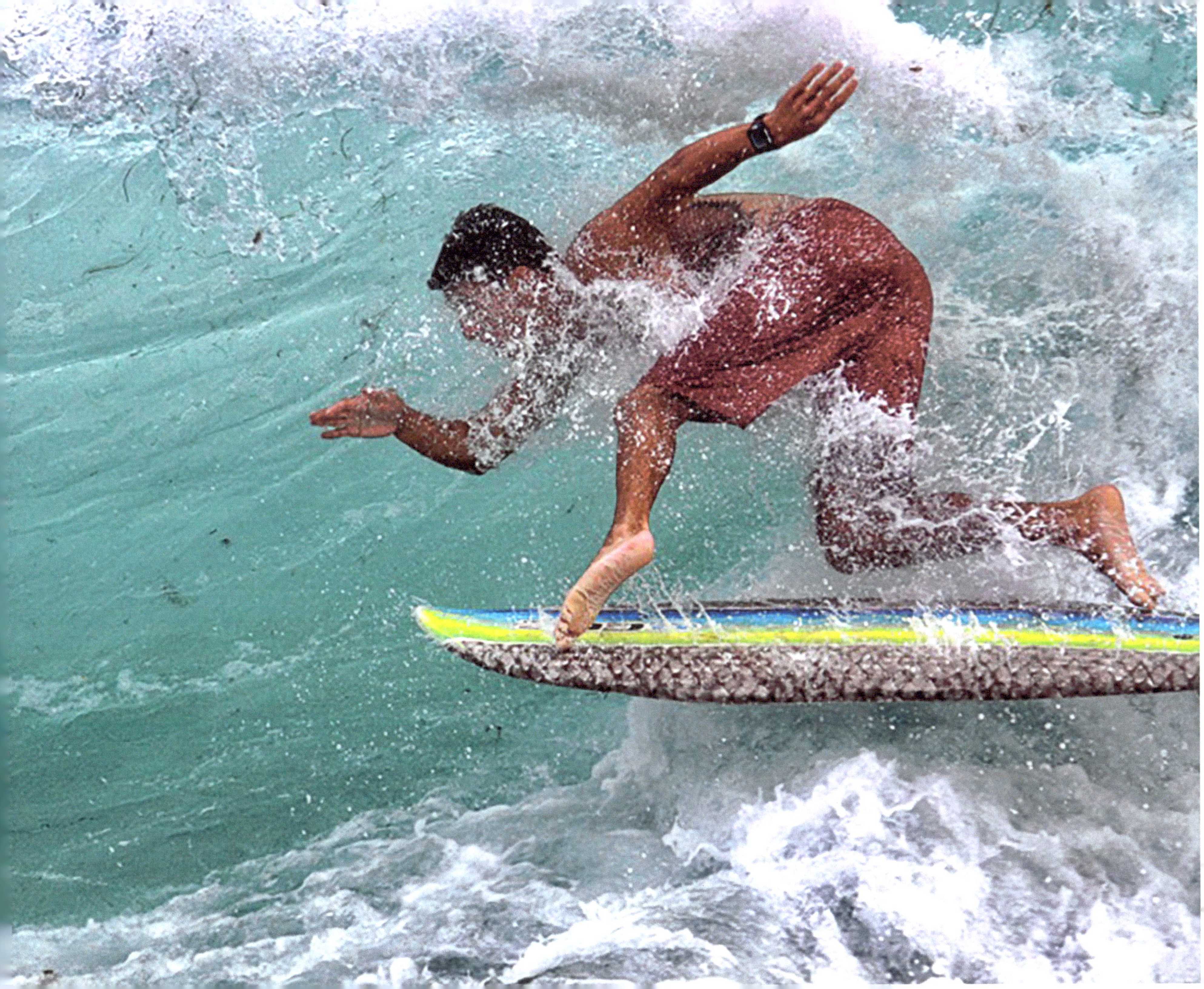

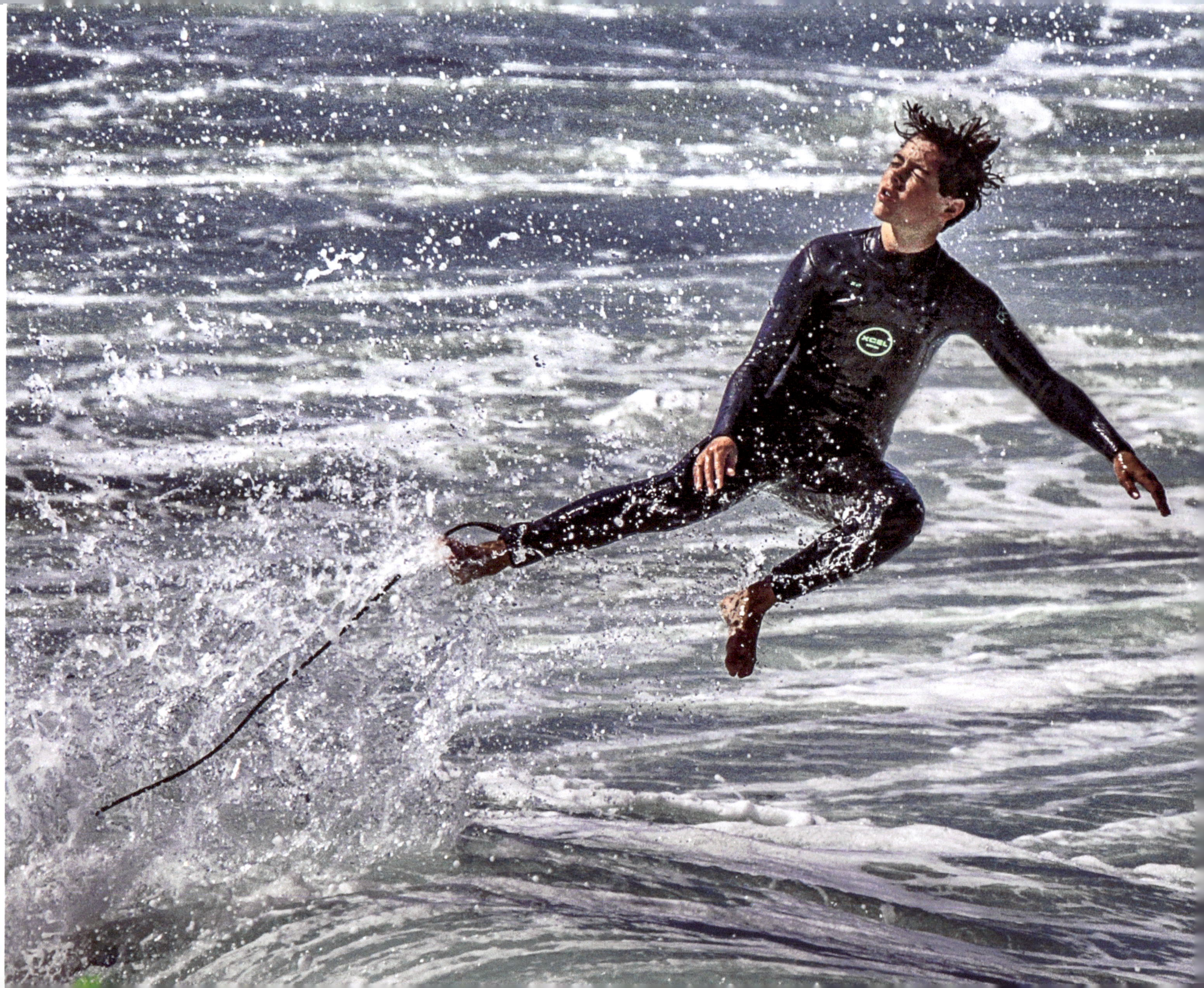

And it got worse. Wayne Land was the one who would pee in bottles and go 'Here, have a beer!' He did that a lot so finally one day I said to myself 'You know what? I'm not doing this shit anymore,' so I got some douche powder and I put it in his Coca-Cola. He rolled around in bed all day in total agony, going 'Oooohhhhh!' I thought I might have killed him. I mean nobody was safe that summer."

"Warning!! WindanSea May Be Hazardous To Tourists."

In the summer of '65, writer Tom Wolfe journeyed out from the East coast to take a look. He was so enchanted by the rebellious surfer subculture and the surf rats who hung out there, that he wrote a story about them called, *The Pump House Gang*. He was intrigued, watching many of the bronzed warriors take on the tourists—"the Outsiders"—with "the Stare" as they spit on the sidewalk before gesturing to the graphitti on the pump house wall, "Warning!! WindanSea May Be Hazardous To Tourists." Some were the

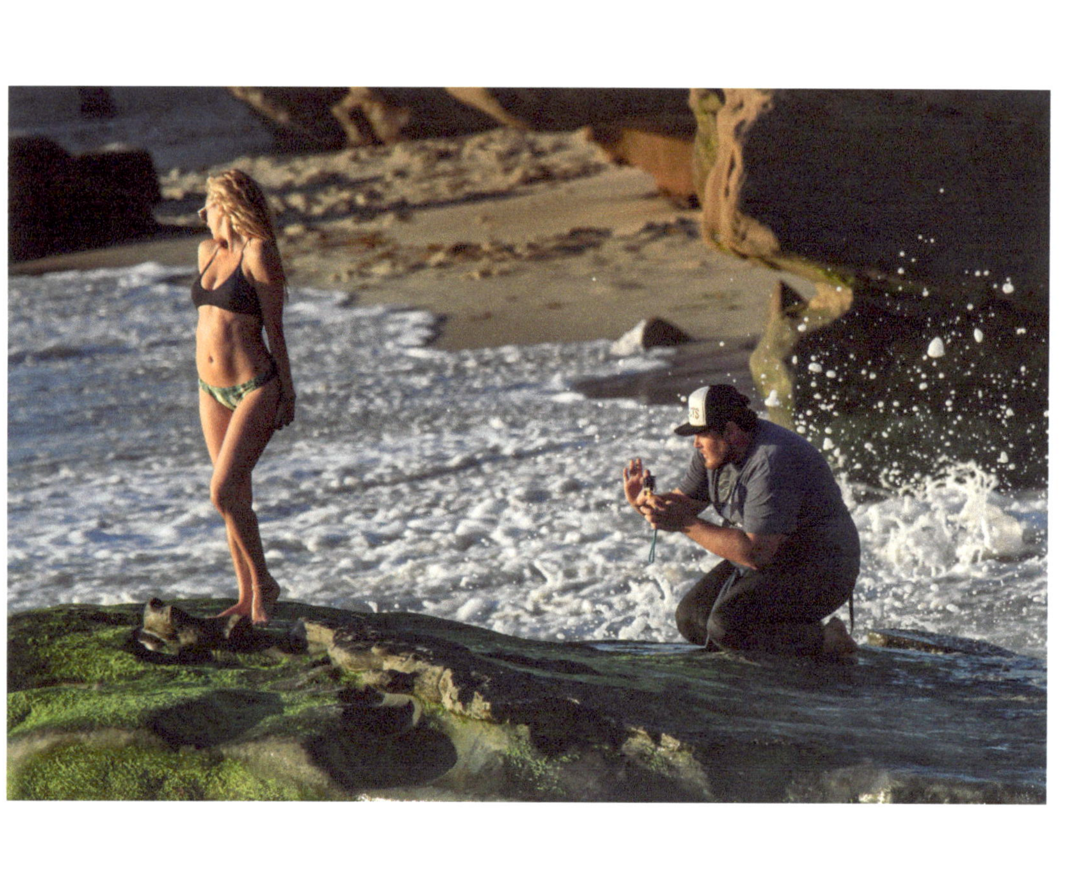

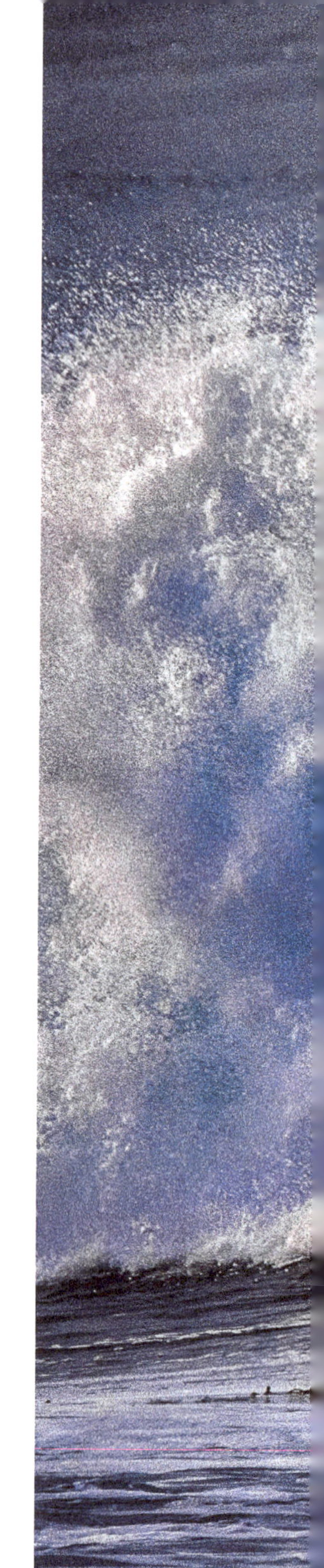

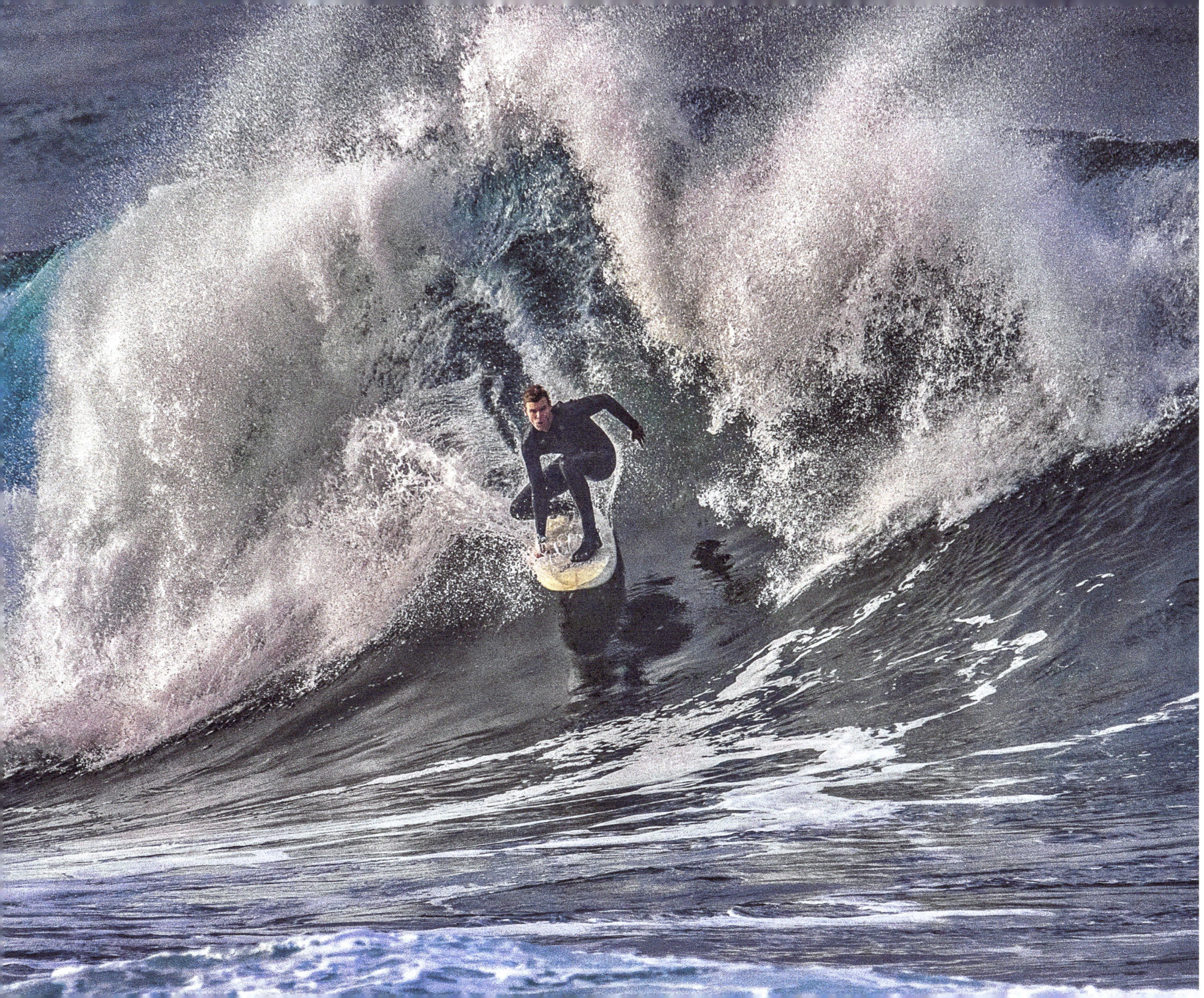

kind of kids whose only surrogate parent was the beach—the kind of kids who jumped in their VW van and drove to the Watts riots for entertainment as if it were a Rose Bowl game. Some were the kind of kids who vowed to blow their brains out on the steps leading down the beach, rather than grow old past their 26th birthday.

After Tom Wolfe's story was published, many of the WindanSea surfers felt double-crossed by how they were portrayed in his piece. Soon afterwards, there was a new graffiti message on the pump house wall: "Tom Wolfe is a dork!"

Even today, some harsh feelings boil up. In 2015, esteemed *The New Yorker* magazine writer, William Finnegan wrote a book about his surfing adventures, *Barbarian Days*. After an evening of signing books at a La Jolla book store, there was a new declaration spray-painted on the side of the pump house, "Finnegan is a kook." That fabric of localism, tribal loyalty—call it what you want—runs deep.

(After reading this book, I hope they spell my name correctly.)

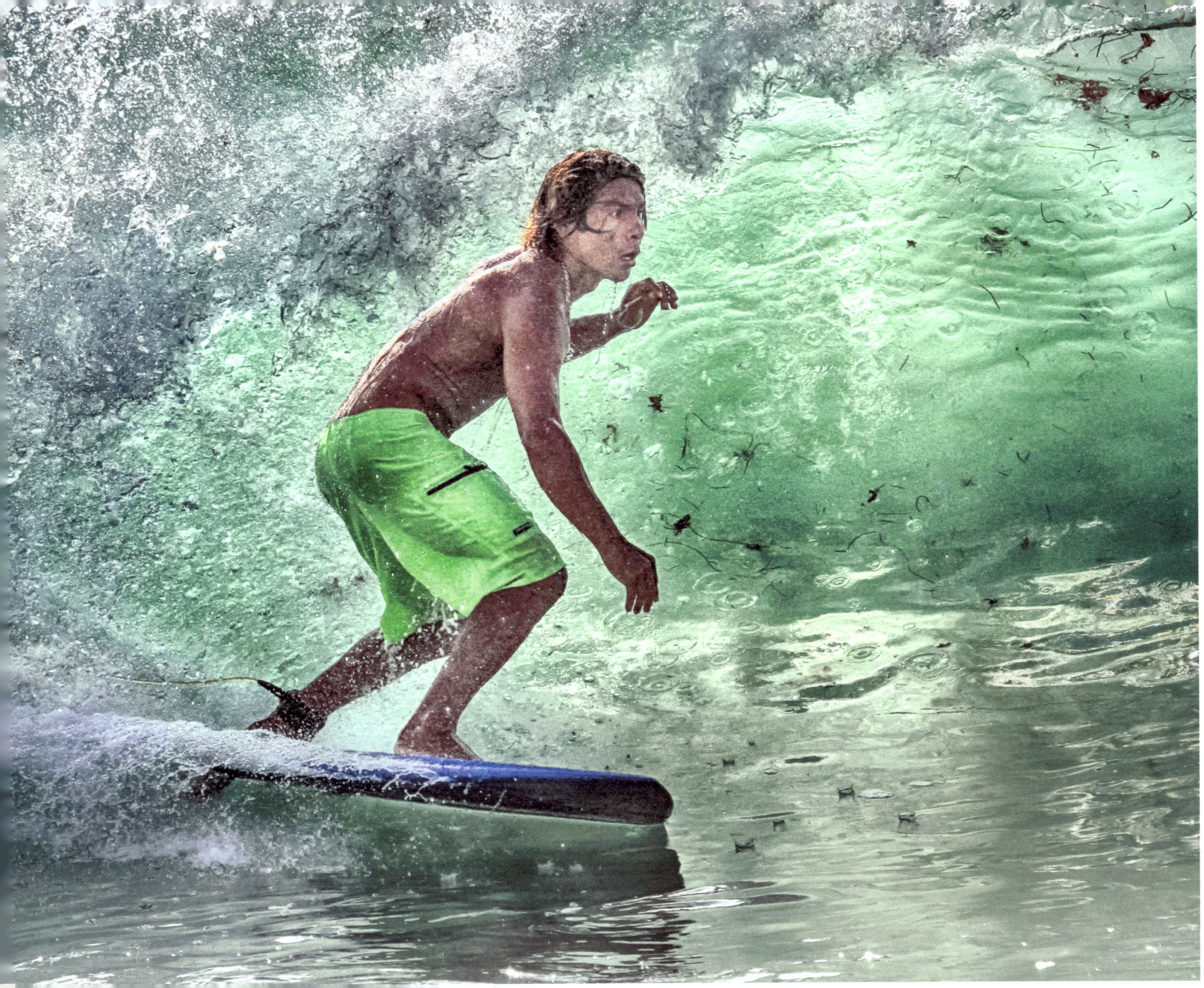

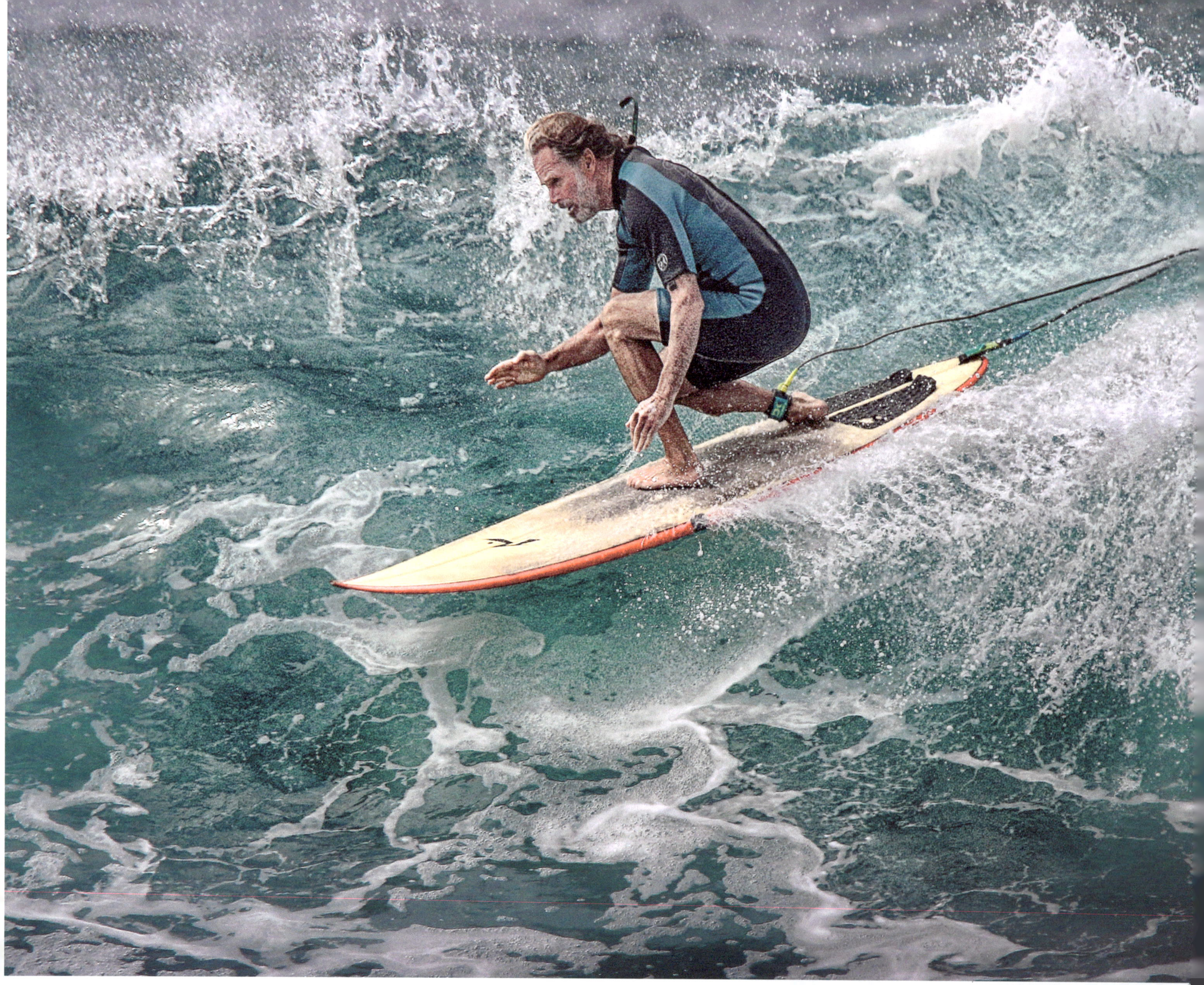

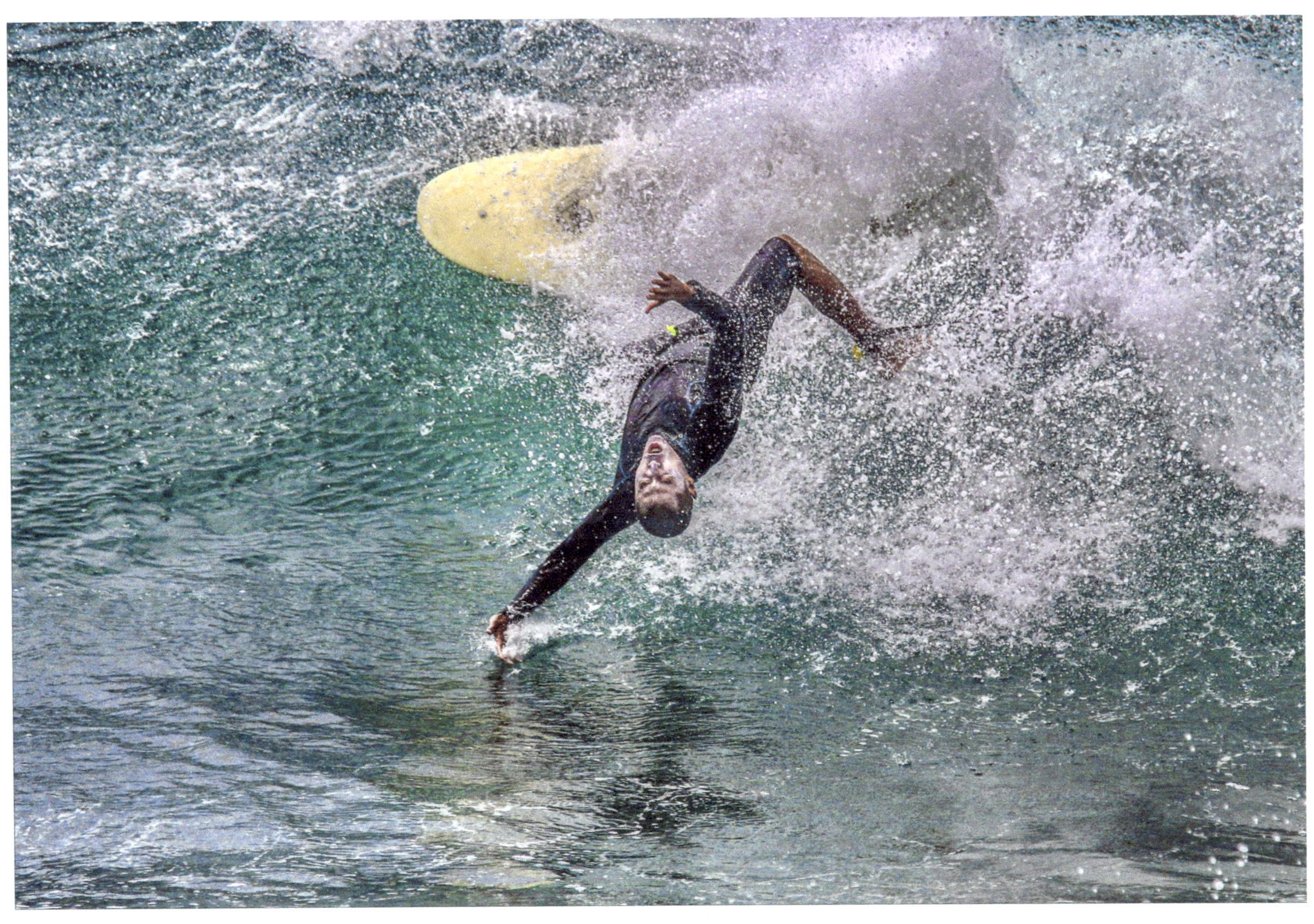

The flip side.

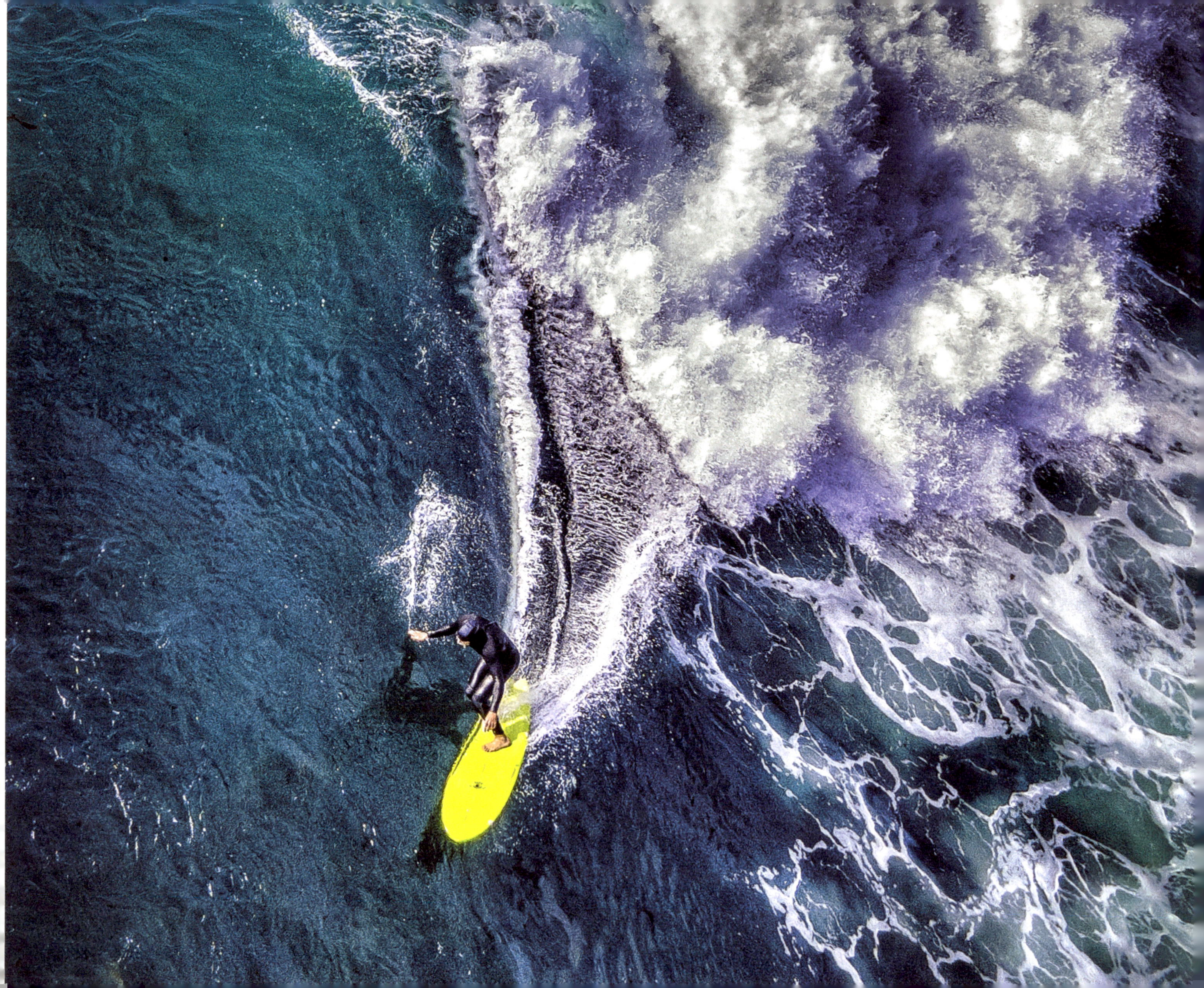

In the early 2000s the equivalent to the Pump House Gang were the Bird Rock Bandits: a group of kids that hung out, drank beer and bodysurfed at the WindanSea shore break. Fueled by a sense of entitlement and booze, they were known to get into fights. Late one night in 2007, during a street brawl, a few of the Bird Rock Bandits killed 24-year old pro surfer Emery Kauanui. A witness stated in court, "They smashed him into a palm tree and took him down. His head hit the street. That was the blow. That was the one." Nearly everyone knew and loved the guy. Emery's murder rocked the community.

"…stories of waves past."

Some visible signs of that era are still etched into a few faces that linger along the short wall of the parking lot. The old timers, beer in hand and leathered pot bellies, slow-cooked from too many decades of southern exposure, watch the surfing below, telling their stories of waves past.

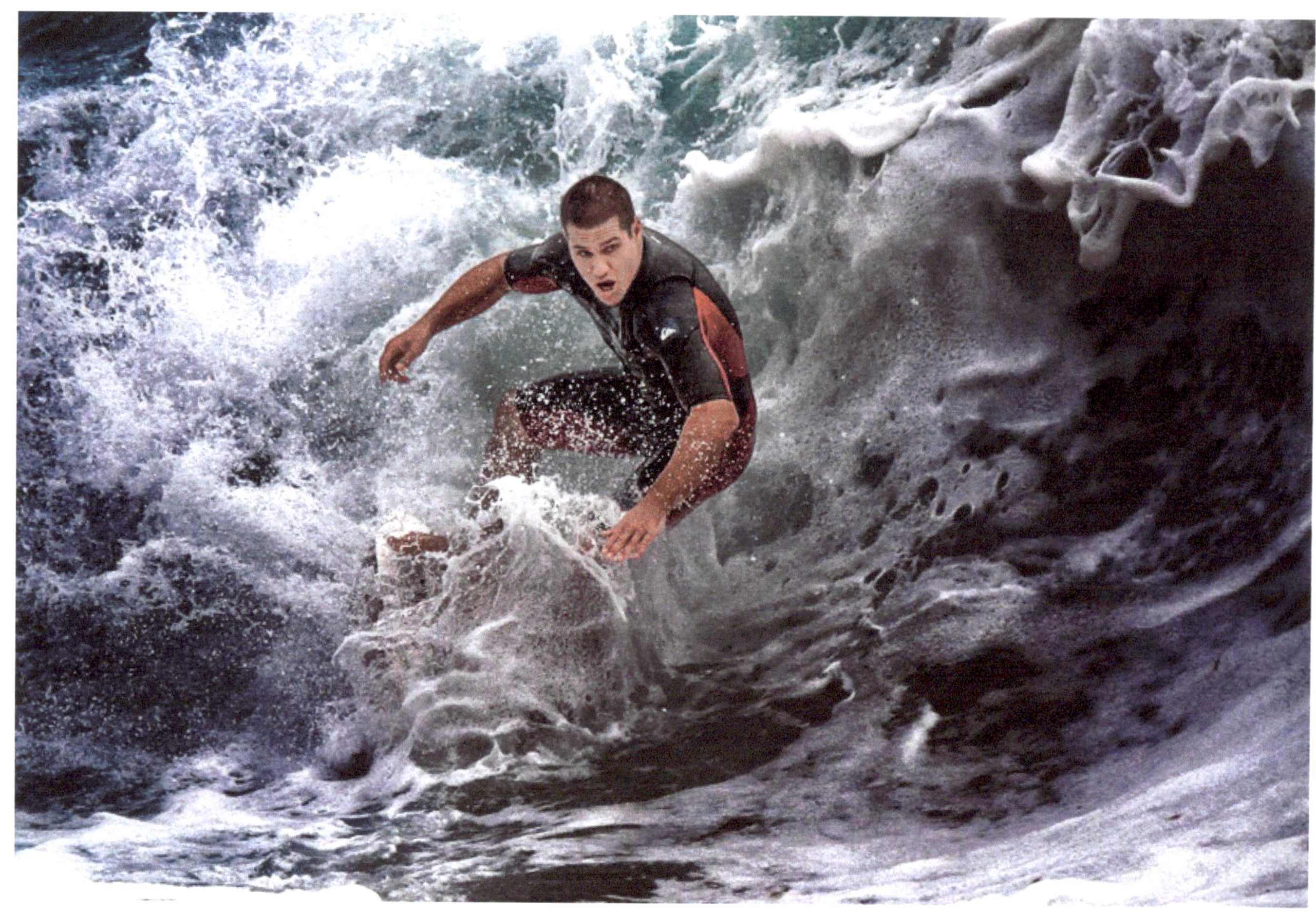

JoJo Roper has chased swells all over the Pacific from Fiji and Tahiti to Portugal and Mexico.
"Surfing just always excites me. I can't get enough of it."

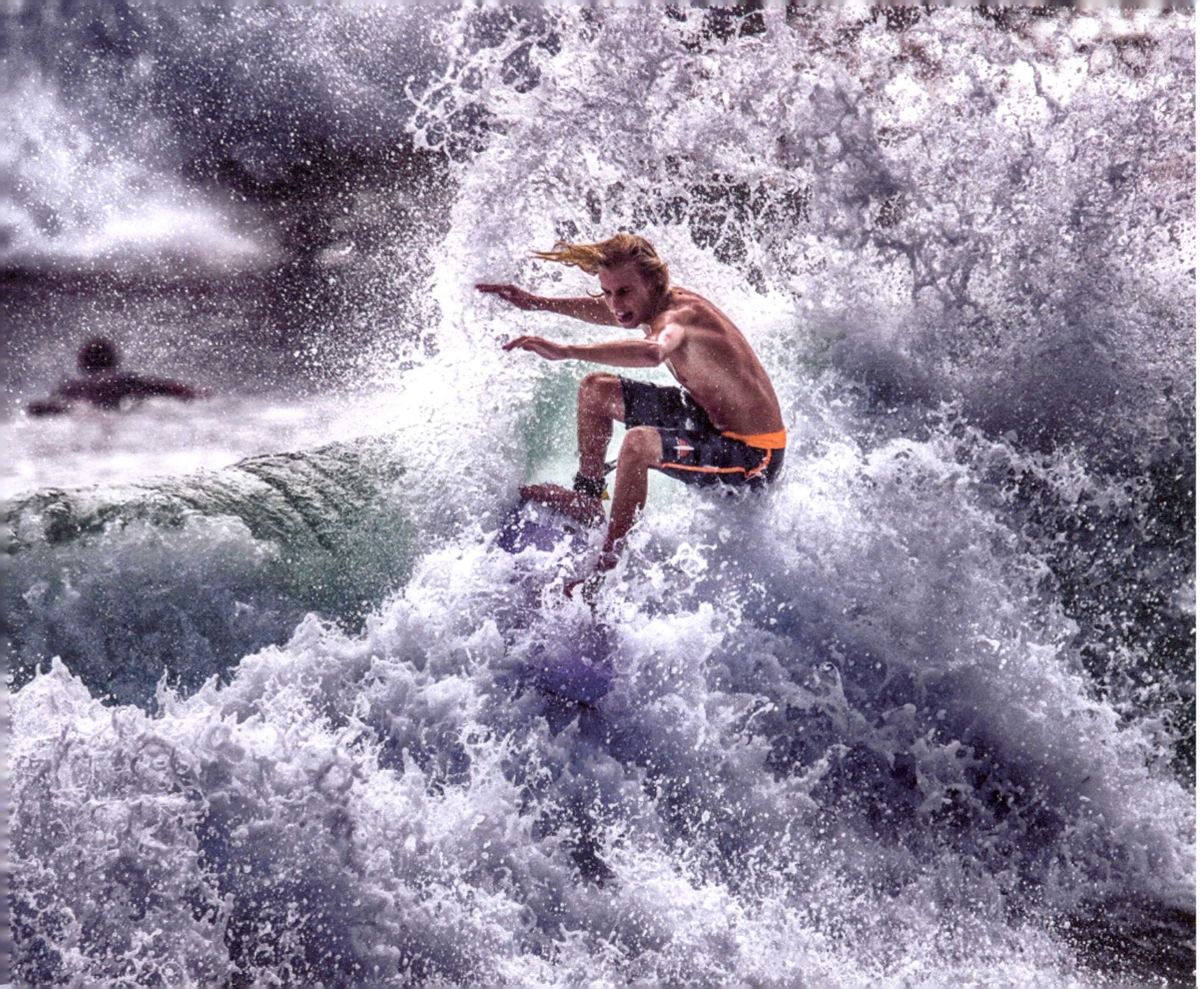

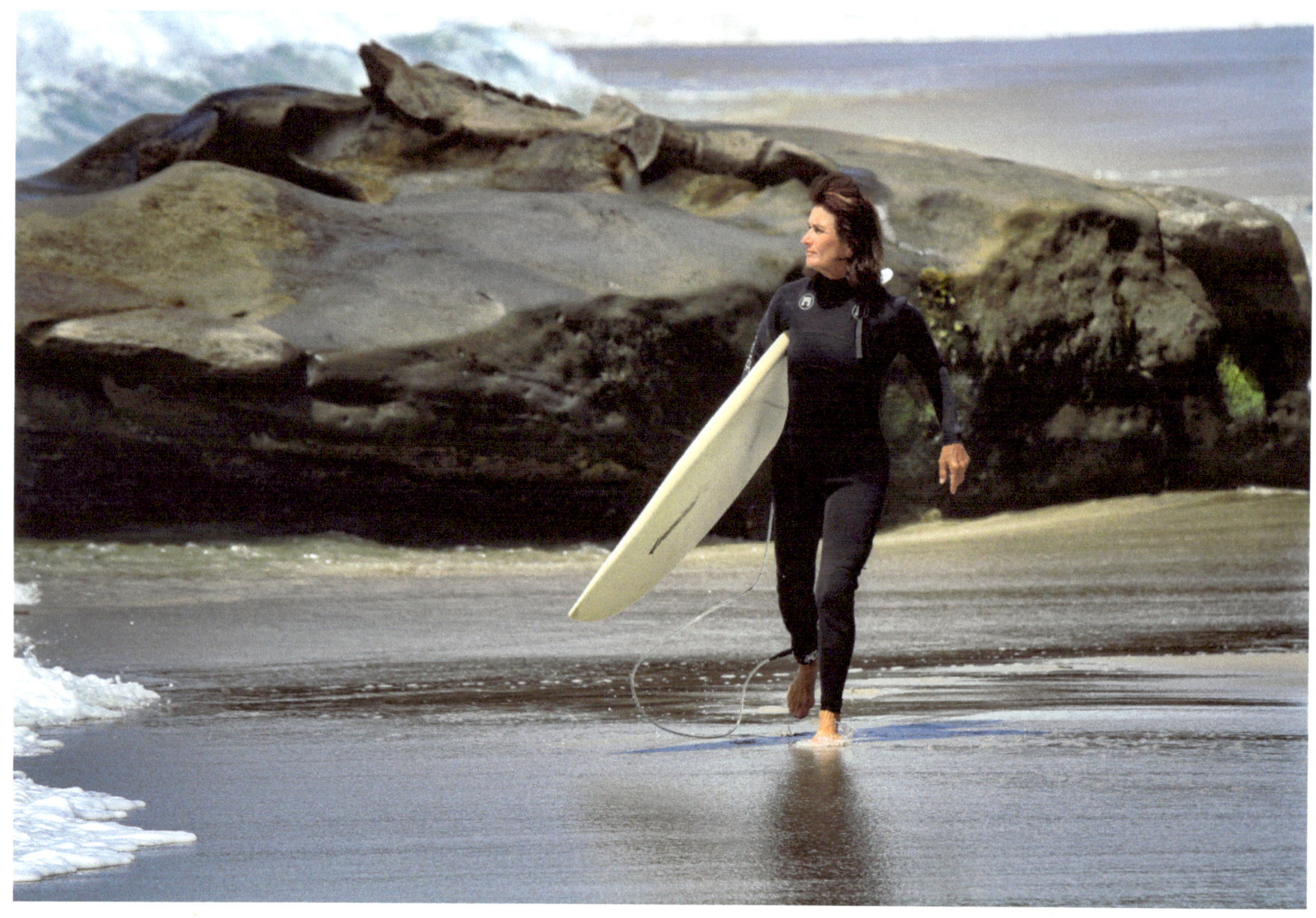

World Champion, Debbie Beacham, no longer competes but she surfs WindanSea every chance she gets.

The light that glows brightly through all of that history is the WindanSea Surf Club. It's a far cry from its roots. Founded in 1962 by Chuck Hasley, the club has included members such as Ian Rotgans, "Big George" Felactu, Longboard Larry, Skip Frye, Joey Cabell, Del Cannon, Mike Purpus, Rusty Miller, Andy Tyler, Tom Ortner, Brew Briggs, Debbie Beacham, Peter King, Saxton Boucher and The Endless Summer film star Mike Hynson. All legends of the sport.

"Debbie went on to reshape surfing history"

Debbie Beacham started surfing when she was 12. She remembers her high school years without much beach drama, telling the La Jolla Light, "The 1970's were such quiet years in surfing, there were very few girls involved. I had my best friend, who was another surfer from La Jolla High School, and we were the only two girls surfing at WindanSea ever," Beacham recalled. "People were very kind and encouraging. Her big brother and all the boys were helpful, 'yes come out! The swell is good!' they would call us.

We enjoyed the camaraderie in those days, it was just so easy-going and laid back."
Debbie went on to reshape surfing history—especially for women—by winning the
world tour event at Bells Beach, Australia in 1982. Beacham later was given the local
Woman of the Year award and was inducted into the Huntington Beach Surfing Walk
of Fame then was chosen to serve as a Vice President for the International Surfing
Association. She still holds the position.

"...groms perch atop the rocks"

The WindanSea Surf Club is the steward of the flame that burns here. On any given
day, fathers with their young daughters run with wax-heavy surfboards into the white
surf. Golden haired 10-year-old groms perch atop the rocks, scanning the lineup for
open peaks, plotting their way for the easiest way to get to them. Men and women
who can get a senior citizen discount at the movies instead ride their longboards
with ease and grace. WindanSea is a mix of multi-generations and multi-cultures.

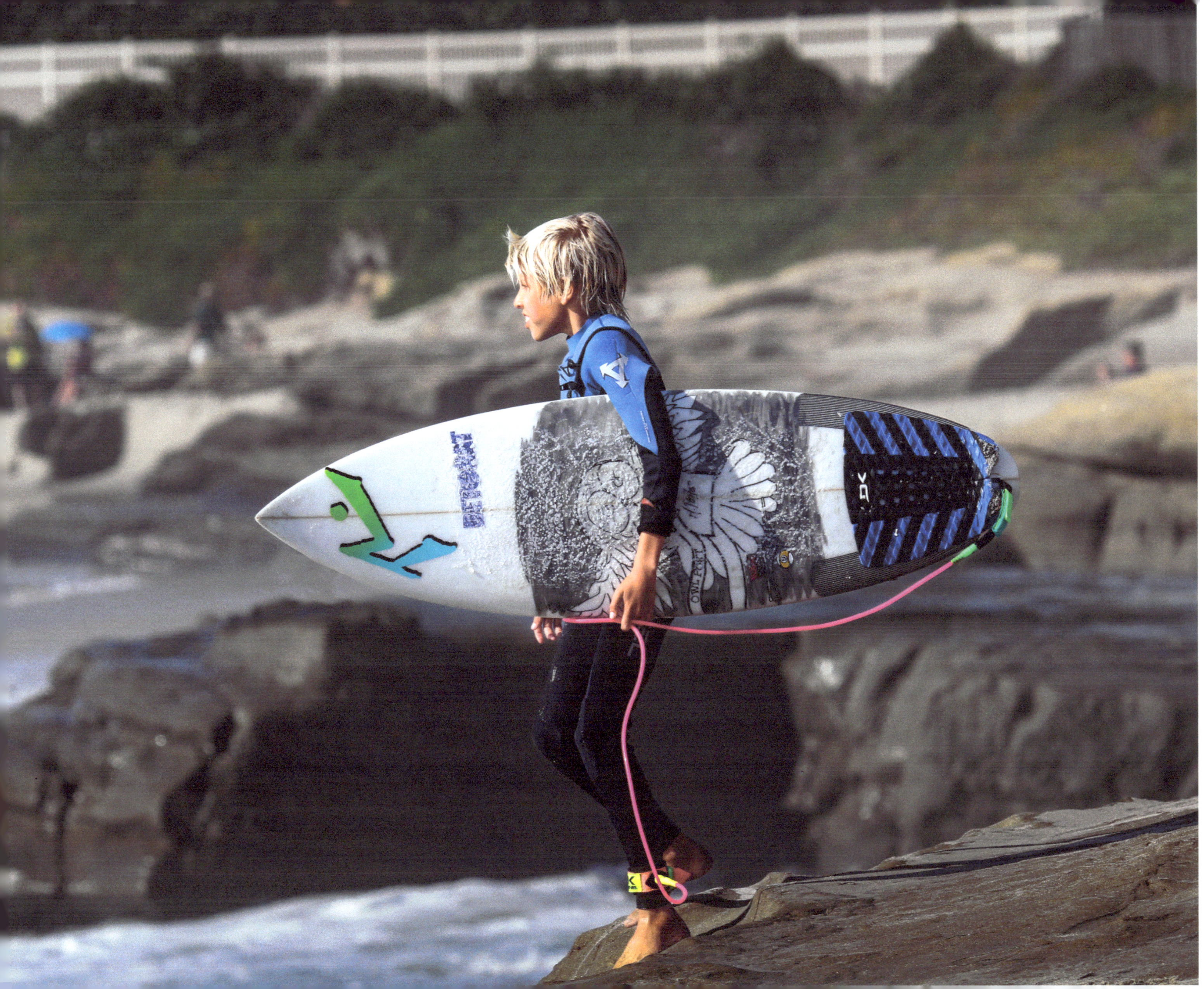

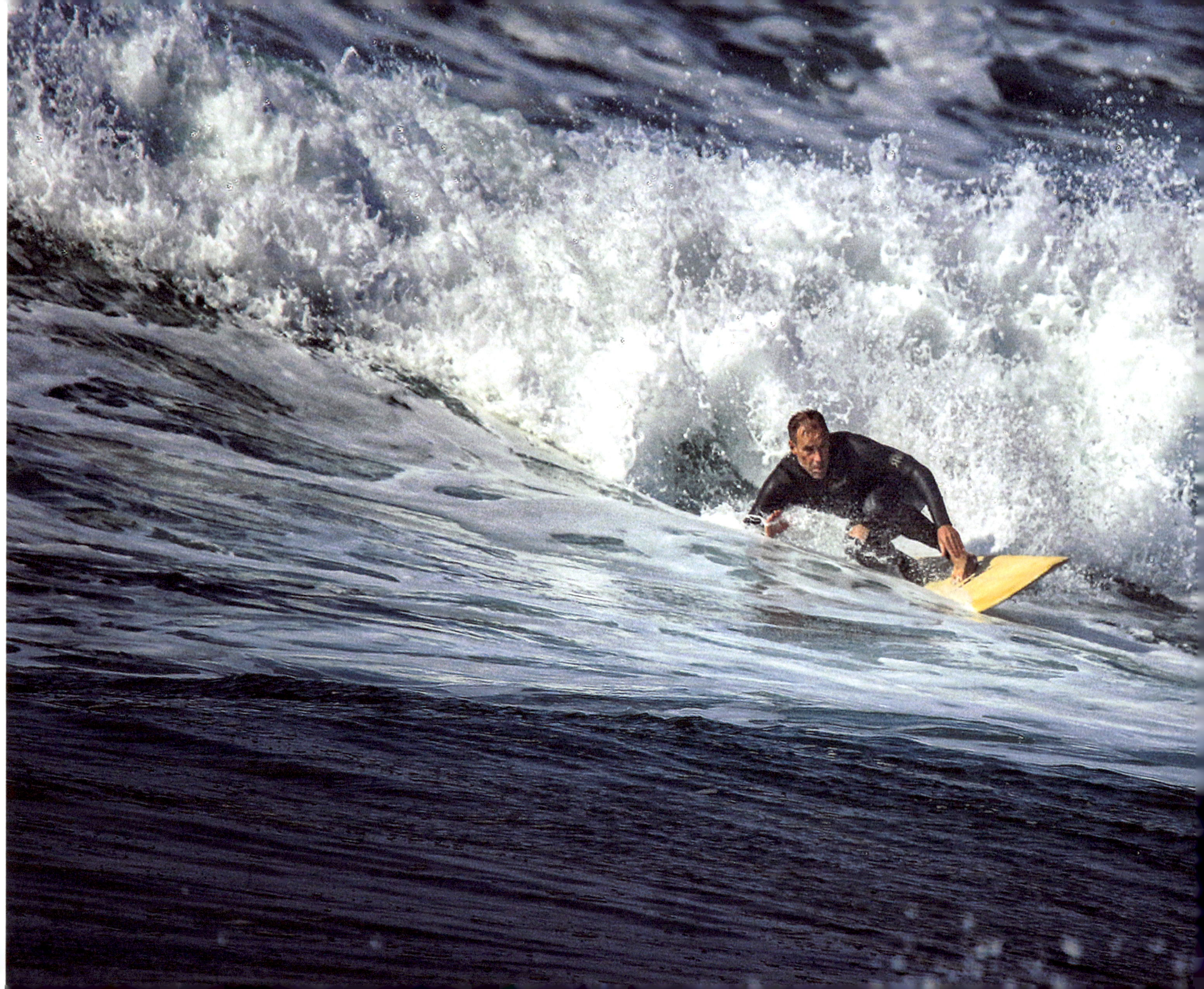

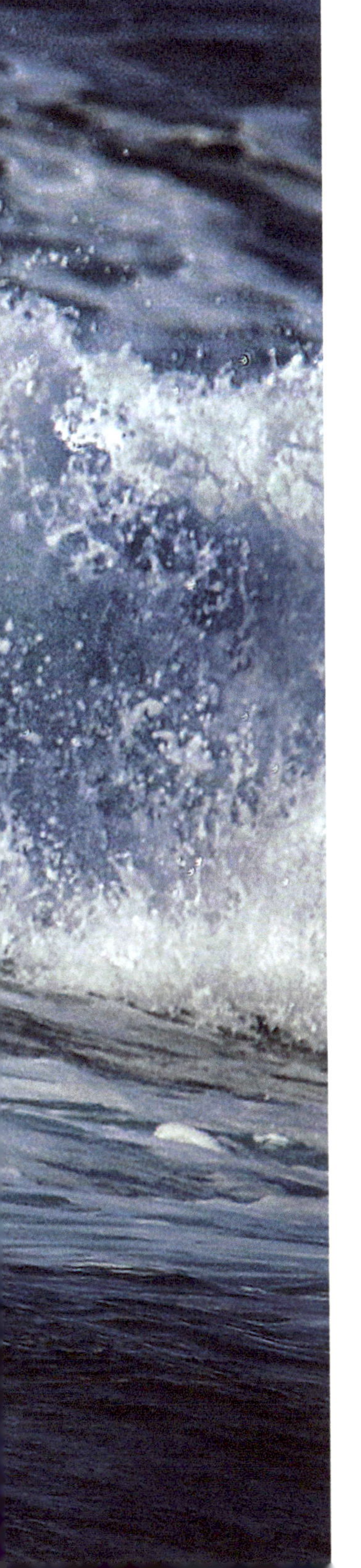
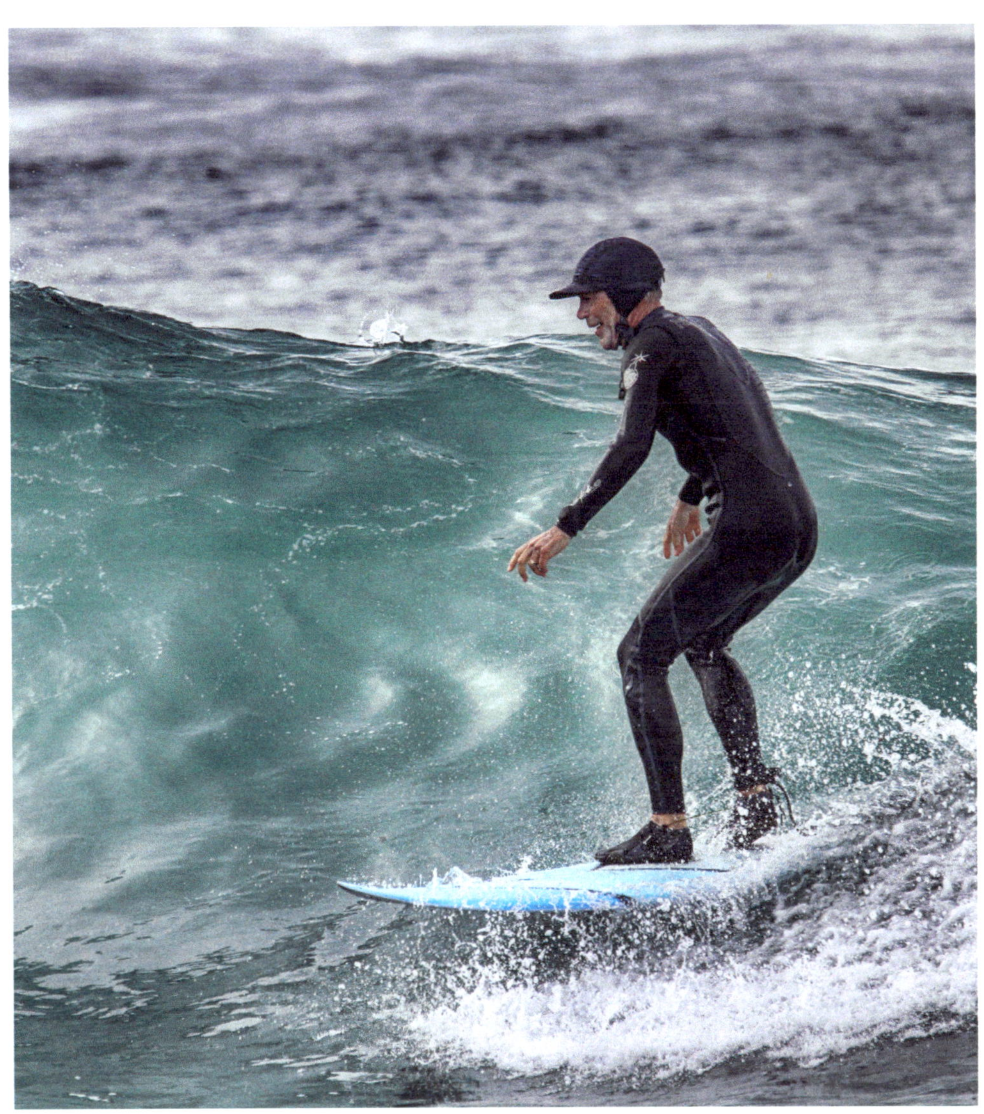

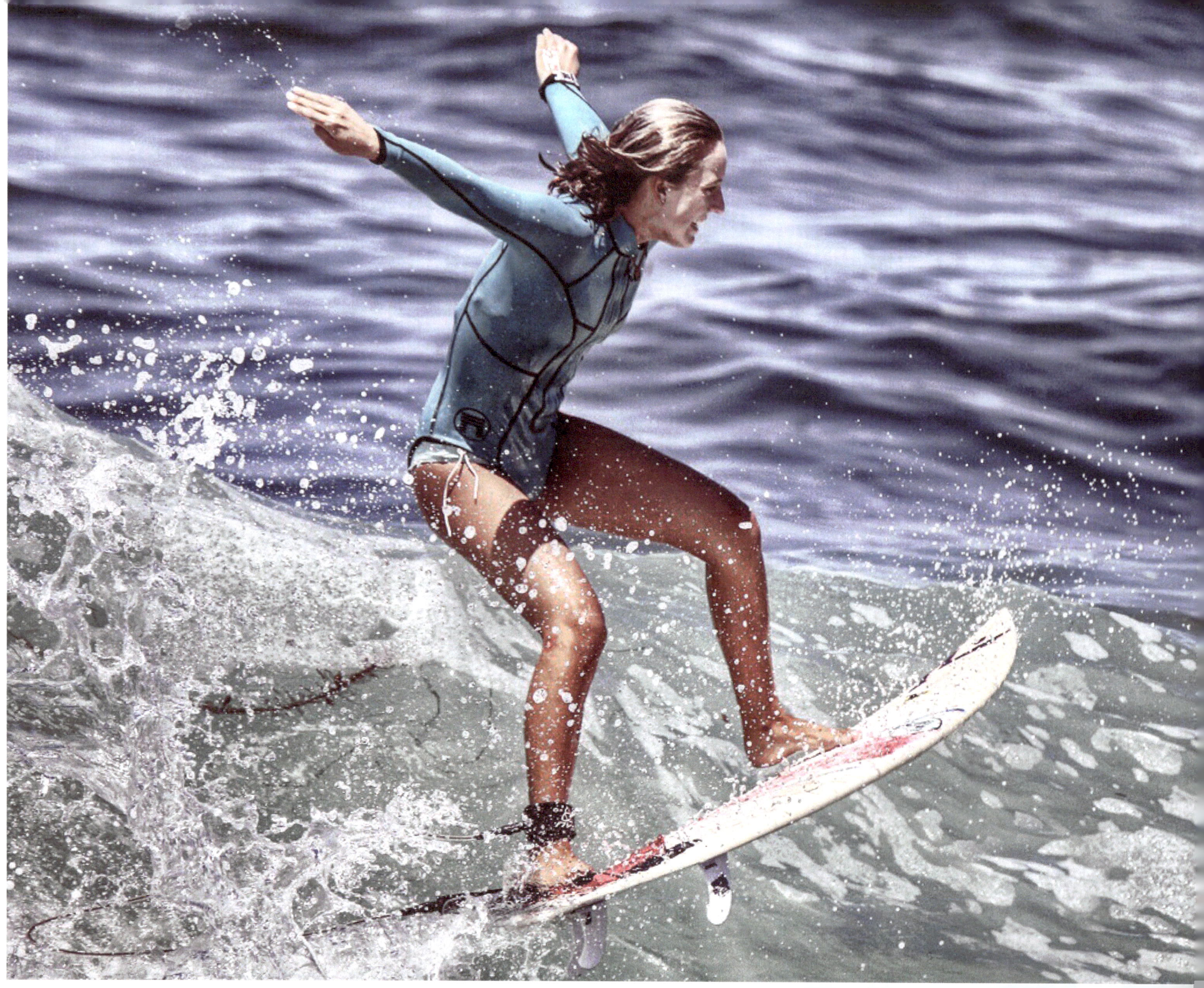

Surf contests are held regularly. On many Sundays or holidays, long tables covered with a smorgasbord of foods greet neighbors, their white table cloths flapping in the breeze. The surf rats who survived the earlier years of drunken fistfights grew up and have mellowed out. Along the way, they found success in businesses, raised families and now find meaning in dedicating their club to "fostering a positive image of surfers locally and globally through charity and competition, and supporting our youth for a brighter future."

"a small mountain of liquid fun."

Surfing is one of the oldest sports in the world. It has been around for hundreds of years, from part of a Polynesian culture, to Captain James Cook, to Mark Twain, to Duke Kahanamoku, to Gidget, to Kelly Slater, to Debbie Beacham, to the groms who stand on the rocks at WindanSea. It requires a unique blend of athletic skills and a zen-like understanding of the power of nature and the energy that moves across the ocean, forming a shifting shape—a small mountain of liquid fun.

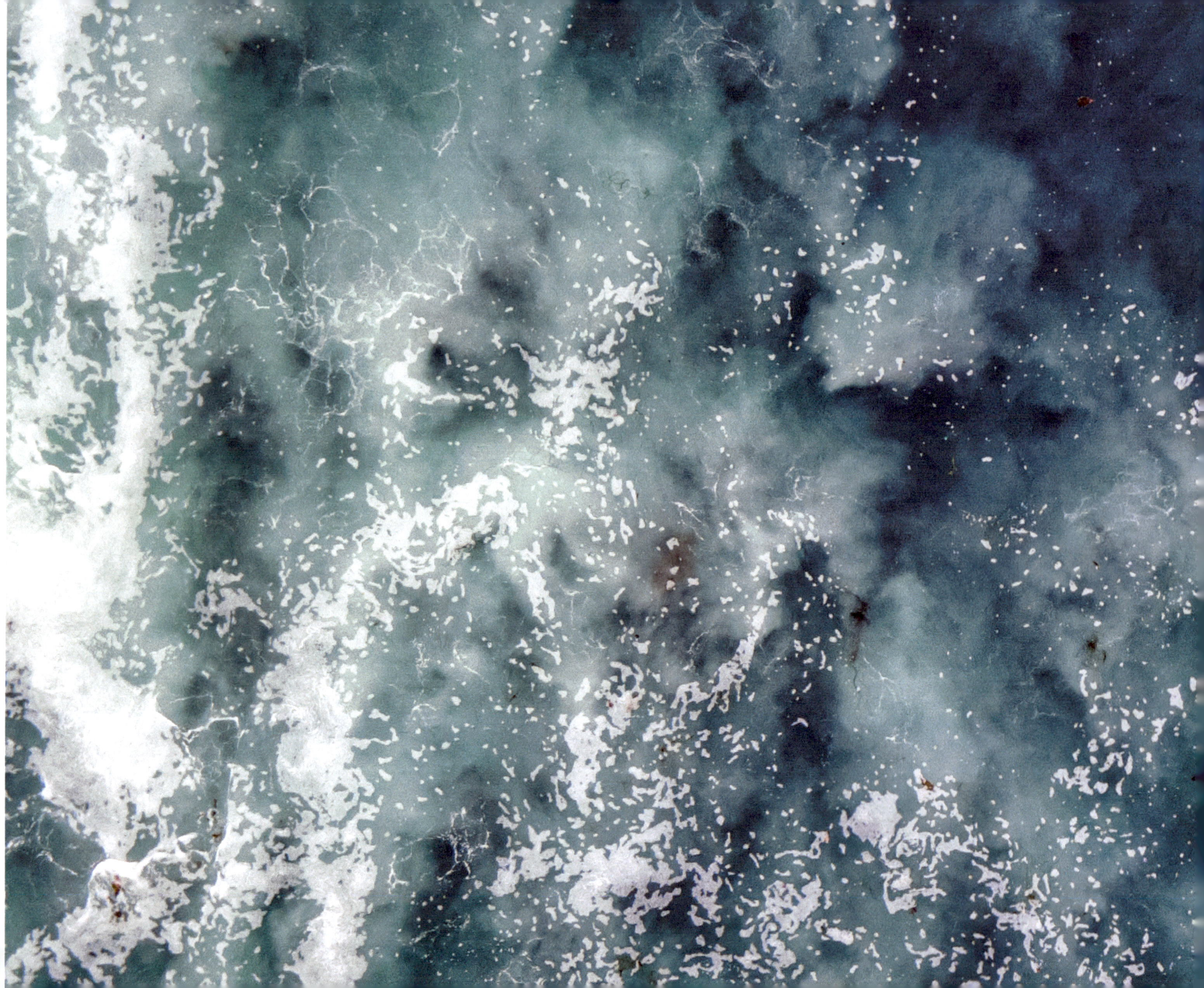

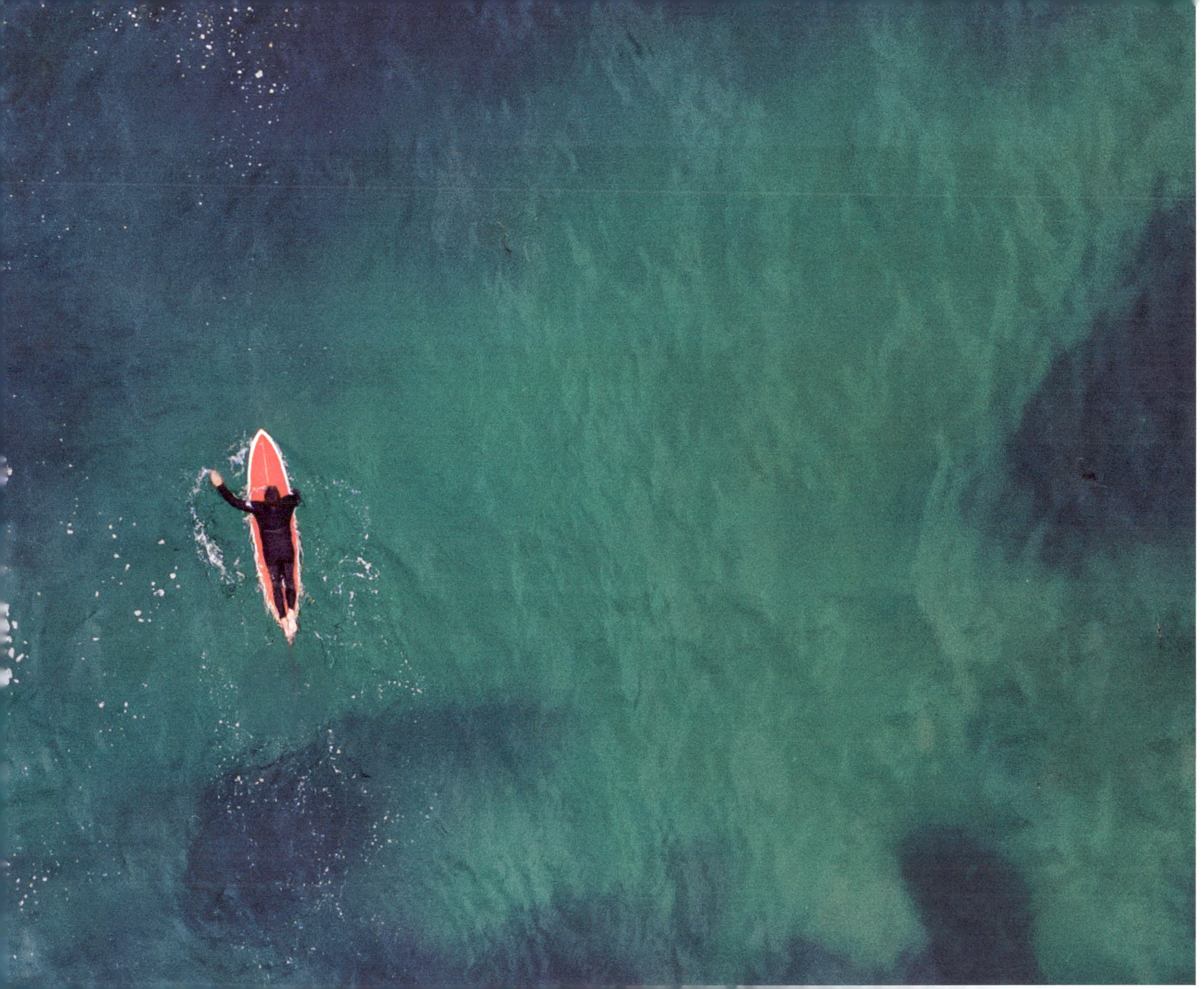

98% of the sport is sitting, bobbing on the board alone while seals, fish, dolphins and who-knows-what swim underneath. Scanning the horizon never stops, squinting for the next wave generated from some weather event thousands of miles away created just for them. Surfers understand the science, the timing, the predictability. The olympians jockey for their place in the lineup, weary that their precious moment on a perfectly formed wave might be stolen. You have to earn your spot, predicated on your skill level, and your history in this hood—all for a chance to be with your god.

As one member of the WindanSea Surf Club told me, "It took a decade for me to be able to join the club. It will take a few more years to be accepted." He later explained, "The worst thing you can do is 'drop in' in front of another surfer, stealing his wave. The second worst offense once you've caught your wave is kicking out too soon, wasting it."

Disobey the unwritten laws of this jungle, middle fingers thrust upward, and occasionally fists still fly.

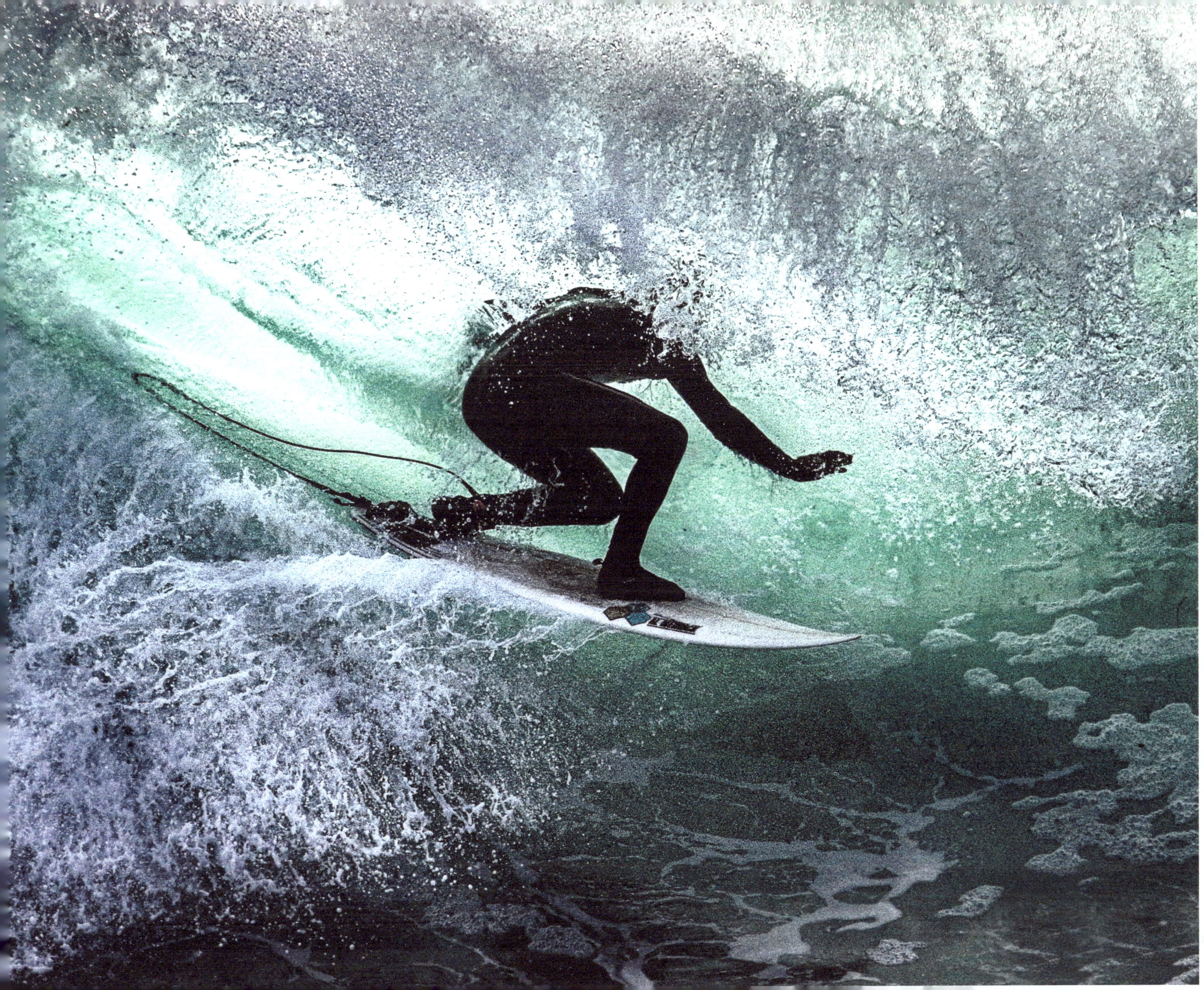

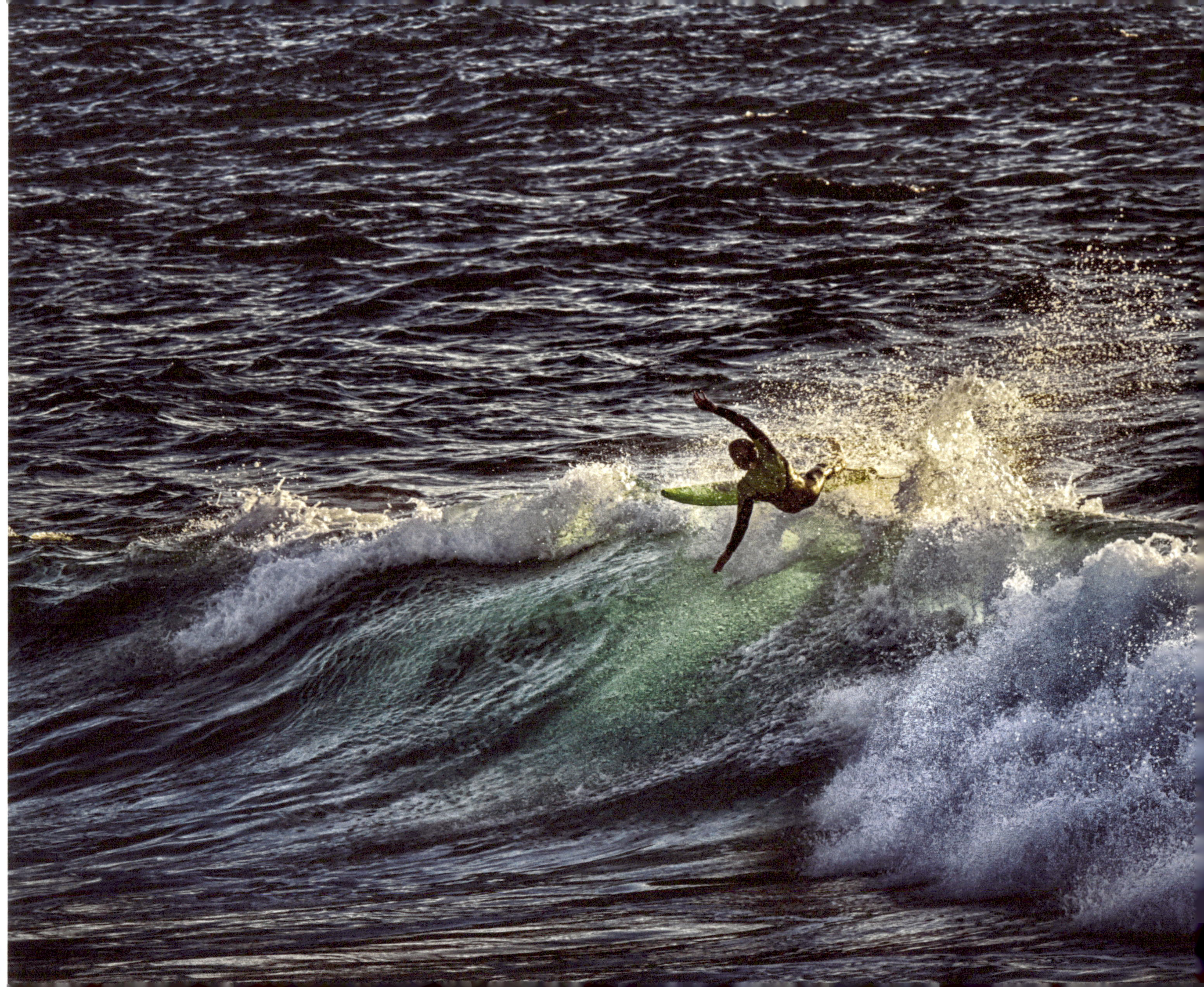

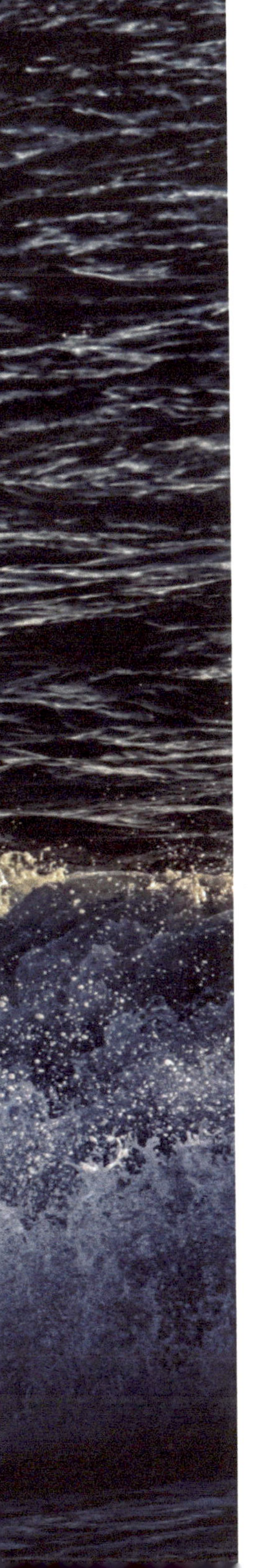

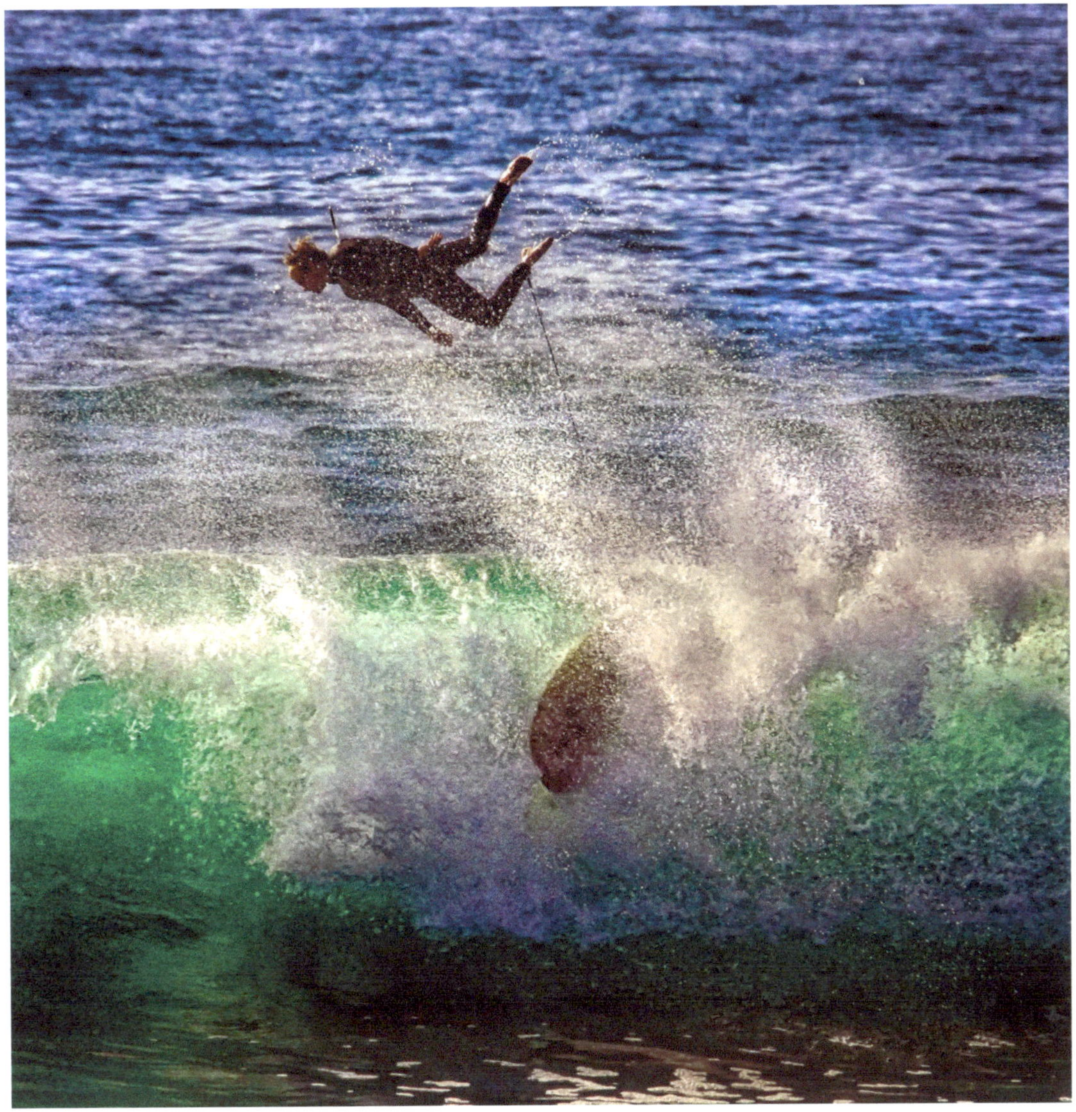

Surfing embodies a passion so deep, no camera resolution can completely reveal it. As I process my photographs after my time at the beach, I'm always amazed at the jaw-dropping skill level of the athletes I've captured through my lens. I am even more enthralled by the the look of unabashed joy and awe on the faces of the surfers dropping down into their waves. I doubt if there is another sport on the planet that telegraphs such electric smiles. The look on their faces answers any questions of why.

An aqua-green wall of water approaches, brushed smooth by the offshore breeze. The paddling begins and the struggle to catch it, ride it, become one with it, get slammed by it, come up breathless, then battle through the oncoming crashing waves to get back out for another round. Once you've conquered your first wave, you don't just want more—you need more. (A surfer once drew a parallel with sex, saying of both, that, when it's good, it's great, and when it's not good, it's still great.)

When the perfect wave finally arrives, the rest of a complicated world recedes. No mass shootings. No mortgages. No politics. No bad report cards. No arguments with your spouse. All your troubles dissolve into the ocean.

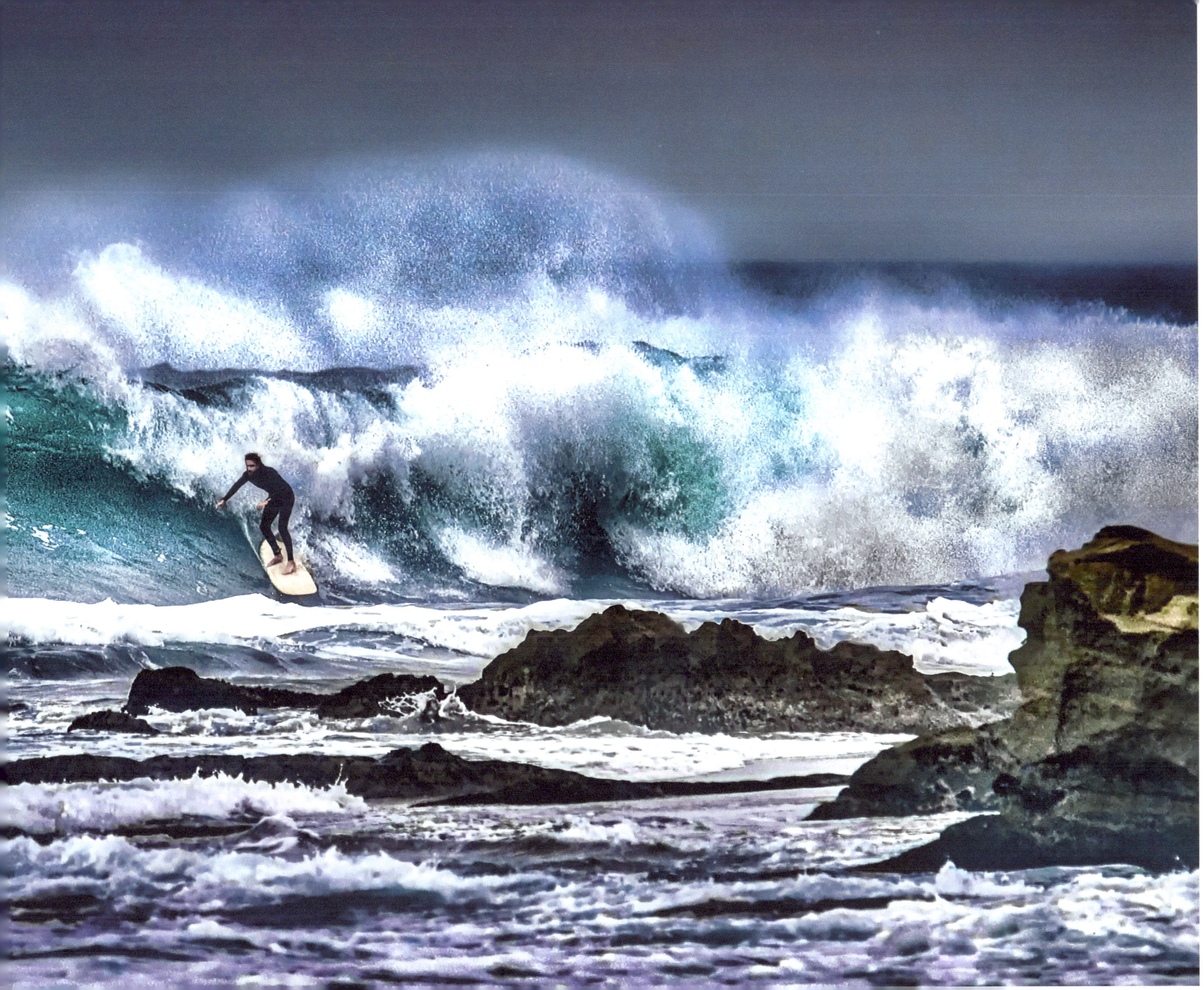

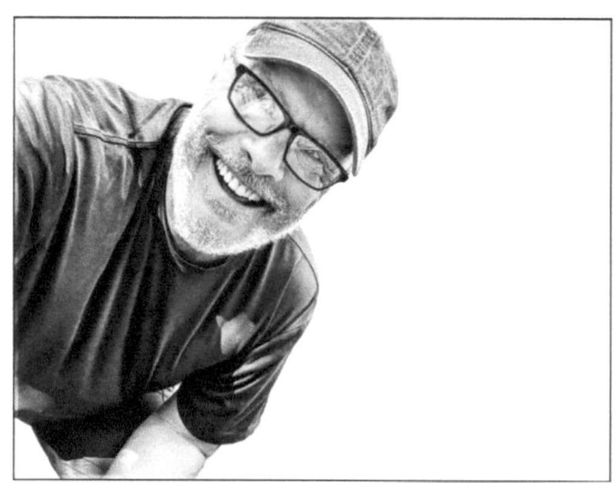

Christopher Briscoe can be reached through
www.ChrisBriscoe.com.